D1271244

The Pascal Lectures on Christianity and the University

Malcolm Muggeridge, *The End of Christendom*,
October 1978 (Eerdmans, 1980)
Donald MacKay, *Science and the Quest for Meaning*,
October 1979 (Eerdmans, 1982)
Charles Malik, *A Christian Critique of the University*,
March 1981 (InterVarsity Press, 1982)
Josef Pieper, *What Is a Feast?*
November 1981

A
CHRISTIAN
CRITIQUE
OF THE
UNIVERSITY

CHARLES
HABIB
MALIK

InterVarsity Press
Downers Grove
Illinois 60515

The Pascal Lecture Series Committee is grateful to the
A. R. Kaufman Charitable Foundation for their support of
Dr. Malik's lectures.

© 1982 by Inter-Varsity Christian Fellowship of the United States of America

InterVarsity Press is the book-publishing division of Inter-Varsity Christian Fellowship,
a student movement active on campus at hundreds of universities, colleges
and schools of nursing. For information about local and regional activities, write
IVCF, 233 Langdon St., Madison, WI 53703.

Distributed in Canada through InterVarsity Press, 1875 Leslie St., Unit 10,
Don Mills, Ontario M3B 2M5, Canada.

Acknowledgment is made for permission to reprint copyrighted material from Plato's
Phaedo by R. Hackforth, Cambridge University Press, 1972, pp. 122-34.

ISBN 0-87784-384-8

Printed in the United States of America

Library of Congress Cataloging in Publication Data
Malik, Charles Habib, 1906-
   A Christian critique of the university.

   Bibliography: p.
   1. Church and college. 2. Church and
education. I. Title.
LC383.M34   1982   377'.1   82-8940
ISBN 0-87784-384-8 (pbk.)   AACR2

17	16	15	14	13	12	11	10	9	8	7	6	5	4	3	2	1
95	94	93	92	91	90	89	88	87	86	85	84	83	82			

FOREWORD

"Perilous times shall come,
for men shall be
... ever learning and never able
to come to a knowledge of the truth."
St. Paul

"What will become of men
who despise little things
and do not believe great ones?"
Pascal

This volume contains the two lectures as delivered, and considerably expanded, by Charles Habib Malik in March 1981 as the third of the annual Pascal Lectures on Christianity and the University at the University of Waterloo, Ontario, Canada. Blaise Pascal (1623-62), the seventeenth-century French academic and Christian, is remembered today as a forerunner of Newton in his establishment of the calculus and as the author of his Christian meditations, *Les Pensées*. Members of the University of Waterloo, wishing to establish a forum for the presentation of Christian issues in an academic environment, have chosen to commemorate the spirit of Pascal by this annual event.

The Pascal Lectures bring to the University of Waterloo outstanding individuals of international repute who have distinguished themselves in both scholarly endeavor and Christian thought or life. These individuals discourse with the university community on some aspect of its own world, its theories, its research, its leadership role in our society, challenging the university to search for truth through personal faith and intellectual inquiry which focus on Jesus Christ.

Few people have the credentials to declaim against the university, which has as long and honorable a history as Western civilization itself, and which (particularly in recent generations) has become one of the two or three most influential institutions in the world. Charles Malik's critique of the university claims an audience on two grounds.

First, Charles Malik is an outstanding academic, having earned a B.A. in mathematics and physics at the American University of Beirut in 1927 and afterwards an M.A. and a Ph.D. in philosophy at Harvard University under Alfred North Whitehead in 1934 and 1937 respectively. In 1935-36 he studied in Freiburg University in Germany under Martin Heidegger on a traveling fellowship from Harvard. Throughout his career he has steadily published articles on philosophical, religious, political, diplomatic, United Nation and international matters, in American, European and Near Eastern journals and magazines. Among the better known of his works are the essays *War and Peace* (1950), *The Problem of Asia* (1951), *The Problem of Coexistence* (1955), and the books *Christ and Crisis* (1962), *Man in the Struggle for Peace* (1963), *God and Man in Contemporary Christian Thought* (editor, 1970), *God and Man in Contemporary Islamic Thought* (editor, 1972), and the *Wonder of Being* (1974). His latest work in Arabic is *Almuqaddimah* (1977). He has also contributed, with others, to more than twenty books and published a twenty-thousand-word article on diplomacy in the 1973 edition of the *Encyclopedia Britannica*. More than fifty Canadian, European and American universities, including Harvard, Yale, Princeton, Columbia, California (LA), Notre Dame, Georgetown, Washington University in St. Louis, Boston University, Boston College, Freiburg University in Germany, and others, have pronounced their approval of his life and work by bestowing honorary doctorates on him.

The second reason this critique of the university can claim an audience is that Charles Malik has loved and served universities throughout his life; he knows university existence intimately from within and feels completely at home in it. In Lebanon he was an administrator of the American University of Beirut as departmental chairman in philosophy, then Dean of Graduate Studies; and from 1962 to 1976 he was Distinguished Professor of Philosophy. After visiting professorships at Dartmouth College and the Harvard Summer School in 1960, he served as University Professor at The American University in Washington, D.C. (1961 and 1962). In his own country he is a founding member of the Lebanese Academy. A member of the International Commission of the Institute of Man and Science, he holds a Gold Medal award from the National Institute of Social Sciences in New York. He is also a Fellow of the American Association for the Advancement of Science, a Fellow of the American Geographical Society, a member of the American Academy of Arts and Sciences and of the Société européenne de culture, the American Academy of Arts and Sciences, the Academy of Human Rights and the American Philosophical Association, among many other learned societies. Now he is the Jacques Maritain Distinguished Professor of Moral and Political Philosophy at The Catholic University of America in Washington, D.C., and Distinguished Professor of Philosophy, Emeritus, at the American University of Beirut.

But the authority which Charles Malik brings to this critique of the university comes from a larger sphere than that of the university, for the Western world knows and reveres him primarily as an international diplomat. He was Minister then Ambassador of Lebanon in Washington (1945-55). He served as Minister of Foreign Affairs of Lebanon for two years (1956-

7

58). He was a signatory for Lebanon of the Charter of the United Nations at the San Francisco Conference for the founding of the United Nations which he attended in 1945. Then he served at the United Nations almost continuously for fourteen years. It was here in the arena of the United Nations that his strength of spirit found its greatest range. At various times during these years he served as President of the General Assembly of the United Nations, President of the Economic and Social Council, President of the Security Council (by reason of Lebanon's membership in the Council), Chairman of the Human Rights Commission succeeding Mrs. Eleanor Roosevelt, and Chairman of the Third Committee of the General Assembly which elaborated the final text of the Universal Declaration of Human Rights which was proclaimed from Paris on December 10, 1948. No person in the history of the United Nations so far has presided over five major organs of the United Nations, including the General Assembly, as Dr. Malik did. The Universal Declaration of Human Rights is the only document of its kind in the history of civilization in whose preparation every nation and every culture existing at the time participated and which was adopted without a single dissenting vote. The great debt that the world owes to this man for his contributions to international peace and human rights has been acknowledged by the more than twelve countries which have decorated him.

It is indeed daring for a man with such credentials and the authority they give him to criticize the university in the name of Jesus Christ. "The question is, What does Jesus Christ think of the university?" he says. "What is the mind and spirit of this agency which dominates the world? The inquiry can be grounded in nothing more final or authoritative than Jesus Christ himself. Every assertion ventured forth here is made in the name and presence of Jesus Christ." This is a prophetic tone.

Yet we cannot deny the history of the university. In contrast to the present prevailing rage against Jesus Christ, the dominant tone at the founding of most of our great universities was a delight in him. "The Truth shall set you free," says the motto of Freiburg University, quoting Jesus himself; "For Christ and the Church" proclaims Harvard in its motto. Their founders saw the universities as a means of glorifying God and of serving mankind through the pursuit of truth in submission to Jesus Christ, the Truth. The briefest research confirms this fact.

In reminding the university that by denying its original purpose it is risking its future, Dr. Malik's words fall heavily on those Christian theologians and professors of religious studies who fail to promote the study of the Bible, living faith in Jesus Christ or an understanding of Christian doctrine. Too often they prefer to accommodate their curricula to the demands of the *saecularis* and of relevance. Yet Dr. Malik does not speak to them as one unaware of the issues they face or opposed to their roles. Throughout his life he has energetically committed himself to service in the organized church and to religious education. The title of Grand First Magistrate of the Holy Orthodox Church was conferred on him by the late Athenagoras I, the Orthodox Ecumenical Patriarch, who asked him to accompany him on his three historic meetings with Pope Paul VI, in Jerusalem in 1964 and in Istanbul and Rome in July and October, respectively, in 1967. He was also made Honorary Rector of the University of Dubuque (1951) and has served as President of the World Council of Christian Education (1967-71). He was elected Vice-President of the United Bible Societies (1966-72) of which the former Archbishop of Canterbury, Dr. Coggan, was president. He was appointed Fellow of the Institute for Advanced Religious Studies at the University of Notre Dame (1969). On formal and informal levels he has been quick to support the three great branches of the Church of Jesus Christ: the Eastern Greek Orthodox Church in which he was nourished from birth and of which he is a member, the Roman Catholic Church and the Protestant Church. In all these activities he asserts his worship of Jesus, saying, "The greatest revolution ever was Jesus Christ himself; not his ideas, not his teachings, not his moral principles, but he himself; for nothing is greater, more revolutionary and more unbelievable than the Gospel of the Crucified, Resurrected and Glorified God who is to come again to judge the living and the dead."

This critique of the university is marked by an informed compassion: for the scientist who, to keep abreast of the overwhelming growth of knowledge in his field, must sacrifice his leisure, his family and his own spirit; and for the humanist who, caught up in the struggle between humanism, rationalism, nihilism, Marxism, Freudianism, liberalism, naturalism, cynicism, skepticism, immanentism, linguistic analysis and a host of other philosophical spirits, finds the beautiful and fragile human spirit tattered, torn, neglected. Academe will not find an adequate check on man's rage for power, not know any sense of order or wholeness, not discover any adequate unifying principle among the many diverse peoples, races, cultures and languages cohabiting the large urban and university centers of the West, not ever resolve the conflict between faith and reason, says Dr. Malik, apart from the pursuit of God through Jesus Christ.

In this unrelenting reference to Jesus Christ, Professor Malik echoes Blaise Pascal, also a scientist, humanist and Christian:

Not only do we only know God through Jesus Christ, but we only know ourselves through Jesus Christ; we only know life and death through Jesus Christ. Apart from Jesus Christ we cannot know the meaning of our life or our death, of God or of ourselves.

Thus without Scripture, whose only object is Christ, we know nothing, and can see nothing but obscurity and confusion in the nature of God and in nature itself. (*Pensée* 417) Such a focus will hardly be tolerated within the twentieth-century universities (which nevertheless pride themselves on their toleration). But Charles Malik is not narrow in spirit, or uninformed or insensitive. The exhilaration with which one reads his books or attends to his lectures is partly due to the intensity of his love for individuals from so diverse and even mutually hostile religious, cultural and philosophical traditions, an intensity consequent on his profound understanding of them. Seldom does a man so love those who may not agree with him that he reinforces their strengths while standing firmly in the face of their disagreement: one senses how much he is aware of being loved—and forgiven—himself. It is enough to set one in pursuit of Malik's Master.

John North, Chairman
Pascal Lecture Series Committee, 1980-81
University of Waterloo
Waterloo, Ontario
Canada

PREFACE

I wish to express to the Pascal Lecture Series Committee of the University of Waterloo in Ontario, Canada, and especially to the Chairman of the Committee, John North, my appreciation for inviting me to deliver the Pascal Lectures on Christianity and the University on March 2 and 3, 1981 on the topic "A Christian Critique of the University." North and the members of his Committee as well as the administration, faculty and student body of the University, were gracious to us during the two or three days my wife and I spent at the University. We thank them for the friendly reception they accorded us.

The present book is an elaboration of the two lectures I gave at the University of Waterloo. In the space of two lectures one can only compress the material to a few central themes. Even the present expanded form in this book remains a preliminary treatment of the subject.

The great universities of the Western world raise fundamental questions from the Christian point of view. They are pretty thoroughly secularized. The prevailing atmosphere in them is not congenial to Christian spiritual values. One wonders if Christ would find himself at home in them, and to a Christian nothing is more serious than if Christ is not at home in the great citadels of learning. The questions therefore must not only be raised, but an attempt must be made to face and meet them. Only genuinely concerned Christians who live in the presence of Jesus Christ can do so. This book then is addressed principally to the concerned Christian conscience.

But even non-Christians should ponder the questions, first because Christ is not exactly nothing whether in history or in the world today, no matter how much some people may wish he were, and second because the problems which the state of the mind and the spirit in the university raises are crucial in themselves. At least the intellectual secularists, naturalists and atheists must, if they really care for the truth (and the trouble in the final analysis always revolves around whether people really believe in the truth), stand up and defend themselves. It is never a question of pleasing either the Christians or the secularists but of the whole character and fate of Western civilization itself. Who can be unconcerned or indifferent when this is the question—when it is a matter of destiny and being?

I wish to thank Mr. James Sire, Editor, InterVarsity Press, and Mr. John North for making valuable suggestions to me about the text. I profited from their suggestions. And to Mrs. Eileen Murray, my secretary at The Catholic University of America in Washington, D.C., who labored with me in the preparation of the manuscript for publication, go my sincere personal thanks.

All scriptural citations in this work are taken from the Authorized (King James) Version of the Bible, as printed by the Cambridge University Press.

Charles Malik
Arlington, Virginia
February 25, 1982

CHAPTER ONE

THE PLACE
& POWER
OF THE
UNIVERSITY

THE UNIVERSITY IS ONE of the greatest creations of Western civilization. There is the family, the church, the state, the economic enterprise, the professions, the media and the university. These seven institutions with all their living traditions and with all that they mean constitute the substance of Western civilization. And while in other civilizations there are families, religious institutions, states, institutions for the creation of goods and wealth, a profusion of crafts and professions, and even certain public modes of disseminating information, the university, as universally recognized today, is more distinctive of Western civilization than of any other.[1]

The original model of this institution is the Brotherhood of Pythagoras and the Academy of Plato. All universities trace their ultimate origin to these two ancient Greek intellectual communities. The Lyceum of Aristotle was an offshoot of the Academy. And while, of course, there are universities today in all cultures and civilizations—in China, India, Africa and the Islamic world —these universities, to gain world recognition and respect, namely, to gain admission into the world fraternity of universities, find themselves increasingly compelled to pattern their organization and curriculum after the models obtaining in the Heidelbergs, the Sorbonnes, the Oxfords and the Harvards of the West. Every non-Western university, as a university, has either copied the principles and structural lines of its existence (including for the most part its curricula) from Western universities, or is run by scholars and administrators trained either in Western universities or under other scholars themselves trained in Western universities. The converse is not true: Western universities do not depend on non-Western universities either for the curricula of their schools and departments or for the methodologies of their disciplines. Moreover, non-Western universities cannot hold their own, as universities, except by maintaining intimate, and sometimes organic, relations with Western universities, and by keeping unbrokenly abreast of the immense scientific and scholarly productivity of the Western centers of learning and research.

From Pythagoras and Plato to the present the Western university has developed under autonomous laws of its own, quite unaffected by intellectual happenings outside its own tradition. The original Greek thrust could not have been deflected or substantially modified by the little that has been transpiring in non-Western realms. The Arab-Islamic learning of Baghdad and Cordoba, which helped stimulate the awakening of the West afterward, was itself originally ignited by this thrust. Under the West in this connection I include of course the universities of the Soviet Union because the great Soviet universities antedated the Revolution of 1917 and were all grounded in the university concept of the West.

The reason the universities of the world are Greek in ultimate origin stems both from the nature of knowledge and the nature of the genius of the Greeks. The Greeks, more than any other people, displayed an irrepressible and unbounded passion for the exercise of reason and an incredible curiosity to investigate and know everything; and the university is nothing if it is not the home of free inquiry and unfettered curiosity. "All knowledge is of the universal," proclaimed Aristotle, and this is precisely the inalienable principle of the university. By knowledge Aristotle means scientific knowledge. Thus from the beginning the horizon of thought envisaged by the Greeks was the whole of mankind; they lived and thought in the presence of the unity of the human mind. Man as man was their theme. No people on earth surpassed them, or even approached them, in this.

What you know, or think you know, that you cannot articulate in such a way as to share it with all mankind is not knowledge. It could be faith, it could be feeling, it could be intuition, it could be hallucination, it could be daydreaming, but it is not knowledge. It remains your private property until you manage to convert it into knowledge, namely, until you succeed in communicating it to others, indeed potentially to all mankind. Knowledge is essentially publishable and shareable with all men. Knowledge therefore is not the possession of this or that individual or culture alone; knowledge is never something esoteric: knowledge, as knowledge, is universally human or it is something fake.

Knowledge is the realization of the unity of man as man, and therefore of the essence of all men. Scientific knowledge tells man, every man from Tibet to Timbuktu and from Copenhagen to Cape Town: You have the innate power of seeking the truth of every being, from God to the multiplication table, and of knowing as much of that truth as it is humanly possible to know.

The Greeks, especially Aristotle, devised, and subsequent universities which inherited the Greeks developed and refined, the norms of scientific investigation and communication. The norms and canons are the cumulative property of the sciences and disciplines of the university, and no scientific creativity can transpire in total isolation from them. If we examine the written history of practically every science and every intellectual discipline we shall find that the original conception of that science or discipline was Greek and almost invariably (mathematics excepted) Aristotelian; even on mathematics Aristotle has some very trenchant things to say. Only as we enter into and appropriate the living traditions of the departments of knowledge in the universities can we create scientifically; and this means, whether we know it or not, becoming Greek, or, for the most part, Aristotelian, in mind and outlook. Aristotle is at the base of practically half of Western civilization.

It is interesting to ponder why Chinese or Indians or Muslims or Arabs can enter Freiburg University or the Sorbonne or Oxford or Harvard or Chicago University or Toronto University and specialize and earn a universally respected academic degree in their own Chinese or Indian or Muslim or Arab culture, but no German or Frenchman or Englishman or American or Canadian can enter any Chinese or Indian or Muslim or Persian or Arab university and specialize and earn a universally respected academic degree in his own German or French or British or American or Canadian culture. The reason is that these non-Western universities (and therefore their own native cultures which they themselves reflect) have not yet sufficiently caught the insatiable original Greek curiosity about all being; they are interested in others only to a degree; for the most part only utilitarianly, only to use them, only to learn from them. They are not interested in knowing their essence, their being; they are for the most part wrapped up in themselves; the others are perhaps too strange, too forbidding for them; their original, natural, wholesome curiosity is somehow inhibited.

Western scientific curiosity is so unquenchable (but for one qualification about authentic interest in Christianity which we shall presently introduce) that the West is always complaining against the restrictions the communist and many noncommunist realms impose upon Western scholars and thinkers in their voracious search for the truth of the histories of those countries and the contemporary conditions in their societies. To highlight this feature the West often labels these societies "closed" in contradistinction to its own "open" societies.

More than by anything else, Western civilization is *defined* by total fearlessness of and openness to the truth. To the extent this civilization begins to harbor reservations about this fearlessness and this openness, it ceases to be itself, i.e., Western; and to the extent a society, any society, has developed fearlessness of and openness to the truth, it has become Westernized. It follows that, when we speak of a civilized society, whether Western or non-Western, we are in effect saying, so far as origins are concerned, a "Hellenized" society.

An inhibition of original curiosity has blunted Soviet universities about, for instance, the knowledge of Christianity. Christianity is cavalierly dismissed as so much nonsense or superstition or untruth or opium in the hands of the exploiters and oppressors. Nothing authentic is known or taught in Soviet universities about Christianity; whereas practically everything is known or taught in Western universities about communist doctrine and practice. And, as we shall see, this blunting, inhibiting virus has infected Western universities themselves with respect to the knowledge of Christianity. The non-West is gradually overpowering the West! The original universal Greek curiosity is gradually becoming overwhelmed!

This great Western institution, the university, dominates

the world today more than any other institution: more than the church, more than the government, more than all other institutions. All the leaders of government are graduates of universities, or at least of secondary schools or colleges whose administrators and teachers are themselves graduates of universities. The same applies to all church leaders. How can you create economically without some technical training? But the technical schools which provide this training are some sort of mini-universities, and their administrators and instructors are themselves graduates of colleges, universities or technical institutes. The professionals—doctors, engineers, lawyers, etc.—have all passed through the mill of the secondary school, the college and the university. And the men of the media are university trained, and some have undergone specialized advanced instruction in communication and journalism.

What about the family? In this age of universal education no parents are unaffected by the university, for they themselves are graduates of secondary schools, colleges or universities. And everybody—parents, children, students, professors, administrators, professionals, church leaders, government officials, business people, industrialists and media people themselves —are perpetually exposed to the bombardment of the media. The universities, then, directly and indirectly, dominate the world; their influence is so pervasive and total that whatever problem afflicts them is bound to have far-reaching repercussions throughout the entire fabric of Western civilization. No task is more crucial and urgent today than to examine the state of the mind and spirit in the Western university.

The rest of this essay is for the most part an enumeration of problems and projects to be exhaustively investigated in order to find out the mind of Jesus Christ about the university. This study is a preliminary work. It raises the fundamental question and points out the avenues to be explored in trying to answer it. In the last chapter we suggest, in a most tentative manner, a mechanism that could serve as the means of grappling with the question. Of course the mechanism outlined is a dream; it could even be a fantasy. If an honest Christian critique of the university could come up with a better suggestion, more modest and more practicable, I would yield to it at once. The question is of such magnitude that merely to raise it is not enough: by the very nature of the task we are called upon to propose lines of action.

If the university today dominates the world, if Jesus Christ is who the church and the Bible proclaim him to be, and if we happen to believe that what the church and the Bible claim about Jesus Christ is the truth, then how can we fail, not only to raise the question of what Jesus Christ thinks of the university, but to face the equally urgent demand: What can be done? We are dealing with the power that dominates the world; how can we then rest without seeking to ascertain where Jesus Christ stands with respect to this power? The university and Jesus Christ— these are the two inseparable foci of our thought.

The following discussion falls into six sections: (1) the identity of the critic, (2) the swerving of the universities from their grounding in Jesus Christ, (3) the sciences, (4) the humanities, (5) some problems, (6) a plan for action.

CHAPTER TWO

———

WHO IS
THE CRITIC?

THE CRITIC IN THE FINAL analysis is Jesus Christ himself. We are not offering our opinion; we are seeking his judgment of the university. This very position itself is a preliminary judgment of the university; for one spirit more than any other characterizes the contemporary university, and that is, that there is no Jesus Christ in himself, or, for that matter, there is no being in itself: there is only our opinion of Jesus Christ or of this or that being.

But Jesus Christ exists in himself and he holds the entire world, including the university, in the palm of his hands. This is a dogmatic statement, of course, but ours must be a "Christian" critique of the university. And those who know him and love him and trust him and seek his presence day and night are granted, at his pleasure, his Holy Spirit who guides them into all truth, including the truth of the university which we are seeking. Do we, however, err? Of course we do, but despite our error Jesus Christ remains and *his judgment* remains, and his Holy Spirit will correct our error if we are open enough to him. The question, What does Jesus Christ think of the university? is valid, and it has an answer. We may not know the answer, but the answer *exists*, and we may expectantly seek it; if it eludes us, it is still there. A *Christian* critique of the university could degenerate into sheer sophistry unless the ultimate reference were to Jesus Christ himself. We are thinking of Jesus Christ himself when we venture to criticize the university. We are not thinking of the university first and then as a sort of afterthought of Jesus Christ; we are thinking of Jesus Christ first, and all along and in his light we see the university. Least of all are we thinking of ourselves and our opinion.

We are asking, seeking, knocking to find out exactly what Jesus Christ thinks of the university. He himself assures us that if we ask, seek and knock hard enough and sincerely, it shall be given us, we shall find and it shall be opened unto us. He likewise assures us that a grain of mustard seed of faith will perform wonders. We take his word on both the grain of mustard seed and on the efficacy of asking, seeking and knocking. In view of the unique place and power of the university today I know of no more important question to ask than: What does Jesus Christ think of the university? All other questions without exception are relatively silly when this question looms in the mind.

To the non-Christian or the atheist or the naturalist or the radical secularist this question itself is silly and irrelevant, because what Christ thinks of the university, even if Christ as such existed, makes no difference whatever to the university. The university is wholly autonomous and follows its own inherent laws of development. Christ makes no more difference to the university than he does to the truth or development of physics or mathematics or the course of a raging war. But to a Christian who knows and believes in Jesus Christ as he is given us in the church and the Bible, and who at the same time realizes the unequaled power of the university in the world today, no question compares with this one.

Since the university determines the course of events and the destiny of man more than any other institution or agency today, it is impossible for a Christian not to ask the question: What does Jesus Christ think of the university? To a Christian this question is an absolute imperative.

I have put it in this form rather than in the fashionably more acceptable form: How do we see the university from the Christian point of view?, because this way of putting the question soon lands us in some form of subjectivism which, as the bane of modern thought, is precisely, as we shall see, what is at stake with the university today. "From the Christian point of view" has no solid foundation unless the word *Christian* here means Jesus Christ himself. So from the very start I have put aside all such questionable phraseology as "from the Christian point of view," "in terms of Christian principles," "applying Christian principles or values," "from the standpoint of Christian culture," etc. In fact it is already a concession to entitle this study *A Christian Critique of the University* rather than simply and directly *What Does Jesus Christ Think of the University?* The real title of this book is this latter formulation.

There can be of course, and there is, a communist or a materialist or a nationalist or a liberal or a Muslim or a Hindu or a rationalist or a secularist or an atheistic critique of the university; and I think I know who is the critic or what is the ultimate criterion of the critique in each one of these cases; but whoever that critic or whatever that criterion might be, in a *Christian* critique of the university the critic can only be Jesus Christ himself. Every word that I say here, if it does not conform to the will of Jesus Christ, I abjure forthwith. And whoever objects to any position or proposition of mine is under equal obligation, if he cares, to demonstrate that it is at variance with the will of Jesus Christ.

In the nature of the case, therefore, this inquiry can only be conducted in fear and trembling. I know in whom I believe and I trust his Holy Spirit to guide me into the truth I am seeking; I do that despite my fear that my many infirmities would stand in the way. The attempt is worth making, despite the possibility of error; for, as we saw, the university literally dominates the world, and therefore no question can have priority over the question of what is the mind and the spirit of precisely this agency which thus dominates the world. If Jesus Christ exists, as we believe he does, the inquiry can be grounded in nothing more final or authoritative than Jesus Christ himself.

Everything depends on this fundamental personal-theological position. A Christian does not seek proofs of God's existence; rather, like Pascal, a Christian already believes in the God of Abraham, Isaac and Jacob, who is identically the Father of our Lord Jesus Christ. He believes in God through Jesus Christ himself, as he receives him in the living church and in the Bible. He is originally inextricably integrated into the living church and the Word of God which is the Bible. And he lives his faith. A Christian critique of the university is not a speculative-rationalist exercise carried out, à la Kant, "within the bounds of mere reason"; rather such a critique must be originally grounded in existential faith in the Holy Trinity; otherwise it would not be "Christian." The faith is derived from Jesus Christ himself in the church and in the Bible, which is the Book of the church; and this means that Jesus Christ is living, that his Spirit can guide us into all truth, including that of the university, and that the critique of the university from the point of view of Jesus Christ himself is absolutely firmly grounded.

If a serious Christian objects to our interpretation we beg him or her in the name of Christ to put forward an alternative one. We may adopt it and forgo ours. The point equally binding on both of us is that if the university is the most determinative institution in the world then we are both under Christian obligation to think about this matter and to try to answer the question: What does Jesus Christ think of the university? Other critics cannot discharge their obligation by only criticizing the present position. Do such critics think Christ is pleased with the university today? Then let them answer our critique of the university where we show in what respect Christ cannot possibly be pleased. And if they think that Jesus Christ is not wholly pleased with the university, then let them articulate exactly where Jesus Christ is pleased and where he is displeased. My primary intention is to raise this question in such a vigorous way as to force all serious and responsible Christians to think it through themselves.

I repeat: every assertion ventured forth here is made in the name and presence of Jesus Christ (a name and a presence which, while we claim them confidently, we nevertheless seek in total fear and trembling). While I respect every man's opinion, neither his opinion nor mine matters; the only thing that matters is whether the assertion expresses the judgment of Jesus Christ; if it is shown that it does not, the assertion will be immediately withdrawn. The first and last formal and material presupposition of this entire inquiry is precisely this position. Otherwise it is an exercise in fuzziness, in wobbly human effort, in subjectivist rationalism, in futility.

CHAPTER THREE

THE SWERVING OF THE UNIVERSITIES FROM THEIR GROUNDING IN JESUS CHRIST

I AM NOT THINKING OF THE church-related or the Christian-oriented colleges and universities; these have not yet attained the stature of the fifty or one hundred top universities of the world, which set the pace and provide the model for all other higher institutions of learning. Nonetheless, the critique I am developing applies in large measure even to the church-related or Christian-oriented schools. For, measuring their academic status, as indeed they should, by how close they attain to the norms and standards of the more prestigious institutions, these schools, which claim affiliation to his Name, hardly demonstrate in practice (how could they if they must achieve academic respectability?) that Jesus Christ has any relevance to the matter and spirit of their scientific research and learning. After all, it is these prestigious universities which, through the unparalleled research they are conducting, provide the Christian schools with all their fundamental treatises and textbooks for their curricula.

A Christian critique of the university will set itself the task,

first, of ascertaining whether it is the case that the greater, more
established and more influential universities were all founded
on and dedicated to Jesus Christ, and whether in the course of
time they swerved from that foundation and dedication. By
"swerving" I mean the changing of the spirit of the original intention. Notice, for example, the motto on the Harvard seal
which pervades all its schools and departments: the words
Christo et Ecclesiae (For Christ and for the Church) surround the
word *Veritas* (Truth). The motto of Freiburg University in Germany is *Die Wahrheit wirt euch freimachen,* (The Truth shall make
you free).[1] How much Harvard, which is perhaps the greatest
university in the world, and to which I am most gratefully indebted for all my higher intellectual training under Whitehead,
Hocking, Lewis, Sheffer, Perry and others, still is true to its
motto with respect to Christ and the church is a question. How
much the original intention of the Author of the motto of Freiburg University, to which I am incalculably indebted for my
discipleship under Heidegger, is still intended by that university is again a question. This does not mean that some of the
most solid research and scholarship in the world is not being
produced today by these two great universities and by others
like them, nor that I would not send my children, students and
friends, as I have often done, to them if they qualified.

People pride themselves on this "swerving." They interpret
it as progress: the liberation of the mind from all Christian-
religious shackles. The word *progress* has many meanings; but
the most decisive of these meanings is precisely to turn one's
back on Christ and the church. Progress is defined as moving
away from Christ and the church: the more we do so, the more
we progress. There are revolutions and there are counterrevolutions; the greatest revolution ever was Jesus Christ himself; not
his miracles, not his ideas, not his teachings, not his moral prin-

ciples, great and novel and revolutionary as all these things are, but he himself. For nothing is greater, more revolutionary and more unbelievable than, nothing is as great as, the gospel of the crucified, resurrected and glorified God who is to come again to judge the living and the dead. And practically all (not quite all) subsequent "revolutions" were only counterrevolutions to that original incredible revolution. We always have in the womb of history and in the heart of man Christ and Antichrist contending. What a mystery!

The forces of this kind of progress have as their ultimate aim to obliterate from history the very mention of the Name of Jesus and his cross. Inquire diligently what the word *progressive* means (progressive person, progressive doctrine, progressive law, progressive attitude, progressive system, progressive tendency, progressive movement, progressive society, progressive culture, progressive country), and you will find it for the most part directed, consciously or unconsciously, against Jesus Christ. There is always something else put forward to make us forget him: justice, science, culture, prosperity, pleasure, serenity, peace. The important thing is to replace him, to satisfy us without him, to crowd him out of existence altogether. Jesus radically disturbs, and the disturbance must once and for all be put to rest. Little do people know that in the nature of the case this is impossible, because this was once tried in a most radical fashion, and once and for all the attempt miserably foundered. The Man rose from the dead on the third day! Χριστὸς ἀνέστη! When progressivism in this sense entrenches itself, no matter how mildly or neutrally or innocently or unconsciously or well-meaningly, in the highest citadel of learning, the university, the matter becomes very serious indeed.

We know that the universities which set a pattern for all other universities were all founded on Jesus Christ, and we know that

that foundation has now in practice become a relic of the past. A Christian critique of the university raises the question of why this has happened. Is it a natural phenomenon? Was it an inevitable development? What were the ultimate spiritual causes behind it? Does it really signify progress? Progress from what, to what? Is it reversible? What are its consequences upon the whole destiny of man?

Is it a necessary condition for these great universities becoming so overwhelmingly leading in all domains of research, learning, scholarship, discovery and invention that they unmoor themselves altogether from Jesus Christ? Are scientific progress and the worship of Jesus Christ incompatible? Could a saint earn a Nobel Prize in science, and could a Nobel Prize winner in physics or chemistry or medicine or economics fall on his knees and say the Credo and mean it exactly as Athanasius meant it and as the church means it today? Is it a mere matter of division of labor, so that the university will attend exclusively to matters intellectual and scientific and the church exclusively to matters moral and spiritual? Does this division of labor make no substantive difference to the very process of science and thought to which the university dedicates itself, and to the truth value of its findings?

Can the university be recaptured for Christ? If Christ is going to be utterly effaced, what or who is going to replace him? In this fateful contest, who is going to win: Christ or Antichrist, the real revolution or the myriad counterrevolutions since?

CHAPTER FOUR

THE SCIENCES

THE QUESTION OF THE demarcation and classification of the sciences has been a fundamental question in philosophy since Aristotle. I shall not dwell on this question here. For my present purposes, by the sciences I mean all disciplines outside the humanities, and the humanities themselves I shall specifically enumerate in the following. Thus I include here mathematics under the sciences, although mathematics, properly speaking, is a borderline case, or falls in a class all by itself. Also the ascertainment of facts, even in the humanities, is itself a science, although every factual determination presupposes some preconception, and the fact of this preconception has itself to be ascertained.

The sciences are thriving as never before. There is what one might call a scientific explosion. Theories, discoveries and inventions multiply by the hundreds almost every day, and the process accelerates. The mind is dazzled and bewildered: it cannot grasp the whole. It awaits passively the surprise of the next invention or discovery even if it does not know, or does not expect to know, how it came about or how it fits into the whole; and this unknowing awaiting, which is nevertheless every day satisfied, indeed surfeited with satisfaction, could, contrary to all science, have the effect of engendering belief in some kind of magic. One wonders which to wonder at more: the infinite fecundity of nature or the corresponding almost infinite power of the human mind to ferret out nature's mysteries and powers. If you are a subjectivist, which most people are today, you are struck by the power of the human mind; if you are fundamentally oriented towards being, you marvel at the infinite mysteries of nature, because after all the human mind itself is a given fact of nature.

I

A Christian critique of the state of the sciences in the university today must raise ten issues.

1. If Jesus Christ is, as he himself says and as the Christian believes, "the way, the truth, and the life"; if he is, as Saint John affirms and as the Christian believes, the Eternal Logos; if in Christ, as Saint Paul affirms and as the Christian believes, "dwelleth all the fulness of the Godhead bodily" and in him "are hid all the treasures of wisdom and knowledge"; and if Jesus Christ is, as the author of the Epistle to the Hebrews declares and as Christians believe, "the brightness of God's glory, and the express image of his person"; then all truth, governed, as it must needs be, by the Eternal Logos, is sacred, and no truth, whatever be its content or order, falls outside his province.[1] The only question is to guard against the confusion of the order of truth, namely, the disorder and falsehood which result from making the secondary primary and the primary secondary, the original derivative and the derivative original.

There is also the problem of the overall articulation of all truth, if man can ever attain that. A truth in mathematics does not belong to the same order as a truth in physics or biology, or as the truth that you and I are mortal and fallible. When Arthur Eddington and James Jeans in the twenties of this century conceived of God as some kind of mathematician, in the human sense of this term, this is of course anthropomorphic nonsense; when the biologists identify God with evolution, or even see him as the *élan vital* "behind" evolution, this too is nonsense; when the Marxists, denying God as we know him, nevertheless set up as their supreme being, without naming it God, dialectical materialism, this again is nonsense. In all these and similar instances there is a narrowing of vision whereby all truth, including the ordering of truths, is tendentiously reduced to some one particular truth; and this is wholly inadmissible.

A Christian can only bless and rejoice in all truth, provided each truth is put in its rightful place (and there is such a thing as a right placing and a wrong placing of truth), and provided no attested truth or fact or being is arbitrarily denied its rightful place in the scheme of things. For the moment a truth arrogates to itself a place that is not its own or denies other truths, it becomes untruth. When a scientist affirms the truth of his science and denies the truth of religion or morality or great art, then, while his scientific truth, so far as it goes, stands, he himself as a person becomes untrue in the sense that he has denied some truth.

2. There is such a proliferation of knowledge and discovery within the domain of any single science that scientists often find themselves incapable of keeping abreast of what is happening in their own field. Knowledge is expanding, discovery and invention are booming, and the excitement is colossal. Nonetheless, we are here in the presence of some kind of evil, and all evil, including this special kind, concerns Jesus Christ; for he

hates evil and loves the scientist. This language is unintelligible and repugnant to modern man, for he does not need anybody's love, certainly not Jesus Christ's, and he is confident he will overcome evil, especially this particular one which concerns science alone, all by himself. The evil here meant is the stark fact that the scientist keeps suffering the feeling that something might be happening somewhere in his own field that he knows nothing about (or that there is some published material he has not yet seen or mastered) but that might creatively inseminate his own research; and if it be retorted that, far from being evil, this is something good, in that it goads the scientist to greater effort in his research, the answer would be that even this greater effort would not relieve the scientist of his ever-standing anxiety all the same lest he be still missing something important for him to know. (This happens all the time to the scientists, and often you hear them say, "If only we had known about this bit of knowledge in time!") All suffering, all anxiety, all human handicaps under which the scientists labor, are modes of evil, and Jesus Christ hates evil and loves the scientists.

Very important spiritual and practical consequences follow from this accelerating runaway proliferation of scientific knowledge so far as "the soul" of the scientist is concerned (the scientist is likely to laugh when you tell him that he has a "soul"!), as Jesus Christ's primary interest is in this "soul." Nor are conferences, meetings, scientific journals and the facilities of computers and other devices, helpful as all these contrivances are, adequate to overcome this evil. The scientist is so engrossed in his own creative research that he has no time to absorb the findings of others; and whatever time he might spare he is always tempted to plough back into his own work. Is the scientist fated to remain (indeed increasingly) bedeviled with this evil?

There may be a strange satisfaction in being overwhelmed

with material or in realizing that immense creative activity is all the time going on in one's own field even though one knows nothing about it. A sense of pride and importance accrues to the field in question and, by belonging, to the scientist. But there is something perverse in this satisfaction because it is bound to make the scientist tense and nervous. The sense of pride and importance is empty and at bottom unworthy: it could be too costly in terms of his own soul and happiness. Why should the scientist be overwhelmed? Why shouldn't he be in his own field absolutely at peace with himself and his material? I repeat, Christ is a being who sees through all empty pride and self-importance and cares first and foremost for the happiness of the scientist far more than for the great discoveries of his science. I ask, what if such a being actually existed who loved the scientist more than the scientist knows and certainly more than he loves himself? If the scientist here retorts, whether coolly or with vehemence: I know such a being does not exist, then the retort to this retort is: you most certainly do not know that, for formally nonexistence of beings is impossible to prove, and materially there have been many people in history, including many scientists, who believed Jesus Christ existed and continues to exist; indeed, by your dogmatic position you have betrayed the first principle of science, to wit, not to pretend to know what you really do not know.

To the extent to which the exponentially proliferating scientific explosion overwhelms and confuses the scientist, let alone the layman, and tends to make him nervous and unhappy, it is not an unmixed blessing either to the scientist himself or to the ordinary human being. It may be strange language to the dedicated scientist that his soul, the integrity of his person, his happiness, he himself, is more important than his science or his sense of pride and self-importance, and that some actually existing being of the nature of Jesus Christ wishes him well more than his science. It may even be a scientific blasphemy.

The question then arises whether it is possible now to stop the scientific explosion or to limit and control it in such a way as to contribute to the individual happiness of the scientist and the ordinary person and not to their confusion, bewilderment and unhappiness. If it is not possible to do so, then an evil principle is at work beyond man and his science. At least then man should be humble in the presence of what is completely outside his control.

II

3. If this is true with respect to the internal economy of any one science, how much more true is it with respect to the possible creative bearing of other sciences, other disciplines, and of life's raw experience at large, on the progress of the science in question?

The sciences cannot develop each in isolation, or at least such development is essentially limited. They stimulate and fertilize and aid one another and enter into one another's constitution. Mathematics bears on physics, physics on biology, biology on economics, and all of them on the political process. Besides, if there is some ultimate unity of truth, then life itself—its trials, challenges, fears, sufferings, temptations, disappointments— would certainly bear on the scientist as a person and also on his science, at least on his scale of priorities whereby he decides what to investigate next, or whether what he was investigating, no matter how important and "world-shaking," was worth investigating at all. If a great explosion of knowledge is raging within each science, and if the biologist, for example, already finds it very difficult to catch up even with what is going on in his own narrow specialization (let alone in the field of biology in general) all over the world, how can he identify what is constitutively relevant to his own biological investigation in what is going on in mathematics or physics or the other sciences? And it is fatuous to suppose that the sciences alone are helpful to him in his undertaking, and that concrete, personal, living existence is irrelevant.

The poor scientist may be unaware of certain findings in the other sciences, critical for his own research, which he may be incompetent to understand or which, under the pressures of his immediate scientific duties, he simply has no time to explore and ascertain. Teams working together can considerably mitigate this difficulty but not completely overcome it. And how does he know that by being so absolutely preoccupied with and absorbed in his own field (as it were, worshiping it), and therefore by missing opportunities of friendship and fellowship and spiritual love and wholesome, free, leisurely and uninterrupted human intercourse, he is not impoverishing himself as a human being and thereby constricting the scope of his scientific creativity? Occasionally meeting people in the club or on the tennis court or the golf course, or at cocktail parties, is a poor substitute for real, continuous, natural, free, grounded human intercourse. Only rooted, stable community existence can satisfy this need. But it is precisely community life, including family life, that has broken down under technological civilization, and as a result not only the scientist but every other human being has suffered. Technological civilization, itself the product of science, is rebounding with gusto on the life and happiness of the scientist himself, a phenomenon to be seriously pondered. How can a product adversely rebound on the producer, a creature on the creator?

How the scientist may profit from the findings of the other scientists and from rooted human fellowship is thus left to some extent to chance and accident—hearing or reading by accident about this or that scientific discovery, meeting by chance this or that person and establishing a wholesome human relationship with him for a few years, hardly ever for life, and never in a manner to found a living community tradition that will pass on from father to son and son to grandchildren.

Jesus Christ, the living Jesus, wants the scientist to be happy, whole, free, entire, integral, creative; he hates to see him laboring under strain, wrapped up in himself, worrying about dark shadows and uncertainties, a prey to accident and chance, unacquainted with the fear of the Lord and the mercy of God. And yet the concrete situation of science and of technological civilization in general militates precisely against this divine will. Fundamental conclusions follow from these observations affecting not only university existence but the whole tenor and quality of contemporary civilization.

4. The question of ordering and integrating the sciences so as to determine exactly what kind of articulated whole they constitute does not fall within the province of any science. This is the task of philosophy, and to the extent philosophy raises the ultimate issues of life and death and destiny and suffering and rebellion, and therefore the question of God, theology must have a say in this ordering and articulating. The overview of the whole is a theological act. The exact character and operation of this act is to be independently ascertained. Authentic theology is grounded, not only theoretically, but personally-existentially, in the deliveries of revelation and the teachings of the church; and the central theme and figure here is Jesus Christ of Nazareth.

What Jesus Christ thinks of the university so far as the system of the sciences is concerned means here how he orders them in relation to himself as not only the *Alpha* but the *Omega* of all existence. They will be ordered according to how much they enable us to "see clearly the invisible things of God from the creation of the world, being understood by the things that are made, even his eternal power and Godhead."[2] As to the determination of the nature of the inner content of each of them and the articulation of them among themselves into the more and the less abstract and the more and the less concrete, and into which is subordinate to which and which governs which, the innate reason of man, as cumulatively exercised on this matter since Aristotle, being made in God's image, is quite adequate to this task, always subject to deviation and error. Here Christ need not intervene. But the one thing Christ would warn against more than anything else is the possibility of the scientist being so spellbound by any creature, including nature (the error of naturalism) and his own reason (the error of German absolute idealism), as to worship it as the Creator. This is idolatry, and if it should happen God would "give him up unto vile affections and give him over to a reprobate mind."[3] Atheism, the denial of the Creator and the worship of some creature, is the besetting danger of the scientific pursuit.

5. The "success" of the sciences is responsible for a tragic distortion. The unwary and uncritical may become so bewitched by the so-called scientific method as to disregard everything to which it does not apply. The tragedy here is that it happens that the "scientific method" has nothing to do with the most important things in life; for instance, with the life and personal trials of the scientist himself. But a Christian critique of the university and of the sciences in the university has all the time precisely these most important things uppermost on its mind.

6. Another infirmity is to suppose that because a scientist is authoritative in his special field, he can then pontificate on the weightier matters of God, freedom and destiny. People quote

Einstein's views on God and man, not from true curiosity about what this particular great scientist thinks of God and man, but with the intention of transferring his authority in mathematics and physics to these lofty realms. Physics and mathematics and the wonders the genius of Einstein discovered in them have no normative value whatever with respect to God and man and many other such themes. If you have a toothache, you do not go to a lawyer or to a musician but to a dentist. Similarly, to know about God you do not go to the scientists but to the church and the Bible, and to the lives and writings of the saints.

III

7. More serious is what happens to the scientist himself. Four things happen to him. First is what I call the pride of knowledge and power. This is the subtlest failing. Because he controls his subject matter, the scientist slips into the feeling that he is a kind of god. People speak of the humility of the scientist; in truth I find very little humility among scientists. They know, it is true; but what they do not know is not only greater but far more important than what they know. They control, it is true; but they are controlled far more than they control.

Would that they had the humility to ponder exactly what Paul meant when he wrote the Corinthians: "For we know in part. . . ." "Let no man deceive himself. If any man among you seemeth to be wise in this world, let him become a fool, that he may be wise." "Knowledge puffeth up, but charity edifieth. And if any man think that he knoweth any thing, he knoweth nothing yet as he ought to know."[4] But who is Paul to teach the scientists anything?!

Second is what I call the illicit transfer of authority. Many scientists think, as we pointed out under the preceding point, that their recognized competence in their own field qualifies them to pass judgment on matters pertaining to other spheres. (This does not apply to Einstein to whom we referred in the preceding point, for Einstein was humble when it came to realms outside his own. What we meant in our reference to him was people's abuse of a great man's opinion, which he had every right to express freely, to bolster their own views which they had already arrived at independently of and apart from what the great man had expressed as a mere opinion. He would probably object to this abuse and ask the abusers not to take him as an authority in the fields they were quoting him on but consult the proper authorities in these fields.)

Mathematicians or physicists or biologists or physicians or engineers or even experts on government often speak on questions of man, morals, philosophy, theology, history, truth, freedom, destiny, trial, suffering, God, Christ, the Spirit, the church, as though they knew what they were talking about; in truth they are no better than the man in the street with respect to these realms. The habit of speaking authoritatively within their own specialties has been so ingrained in them that they appear incapable of resisting the temptation to speak authoritatively also on matters in which they are babes. The spectacle they display then is ludicrous in the extreme. When a great philosopher or theologian or historian or statesman, or a man who has survived, through some grace, great trials and sufferings without losing his integrity, hears them talk, he quietly laughs; just as they would when they hear a theologian or a statesman or a poet or a saint speak with an air of authority on mathematics or physics or biology or medicine. The scientists should humbly acknowledge that there are authorities in other fields too, and should seek them and sit at their feet; and should never pretend to know what they really know little or nothing about. This is the real scientific spirit which human beings (and therefore scientists), being human, can never perfect enough.

Third is the error of naturalism. Because scientists give themselves to nature all their lives they often end up by worshiping it. The really believing scientist who does not consider the fundamental tenets of Christianity (the Holy Trinity, the Incarnation, the resurrection, sin, repentance, the new creature in Jesus Christ, the Second Coming of Jesus, the life to come) nonsense is a great rarity. The scientists who worship nature develop their own subjective faith, their own private interpretation of these doctrines; they do not want to be bound by these "dogmas." Most scientists are sheer naturalists: nature is all in all. Christ, not as a more or less vague moral principle but his very being and his claims about himself and what the church believes him to be, is hidden from their sight. They see only nature and its potencies and processes. And they radiate this atheistic naturalism all around them.

One reason for the remarkable spread of atheism among the intelligentsia of the world is the ease with which atheistic naturalism, through the prestige and power and "success" of science, passes on from master to pupil, without perhaps the master noticing or willing it. Because scientific naturalism is deeply entrenched in the university, the university has become a principal disseminator of atheism.

Fourth, the scientist, wrapped up in and dedicated to nature, forgets himself. The fact that he is "human," in that he suffers, loses his temper, is tempted, often falls, is selfish, is terribly limited, envies, resents, schemes, hates, is caught up in frenzied rivalries with his colleagues, rejoices in the misfortunes of others, is in desperate need for fellowship and love, faces death any minute, often does not stand up for truth and justice, often lends a hand to slander, often is not fair in his judgment of others, often wishes others did not exist and therefore murders them in his thought—all these common human frailties he is as much heir to as any other person. Science cannot save the scientist from them. In fact, like other people, scientists are prone to flee from them. These things are mightily there all the time, but one gets the impression sometimes that scientists pay little attention to them.

These frailties are, to use a Whiteheadian term, mere "subjective forms," of no special metaphysical importance. The scientists as persons are not important (and yet how much they are jealous for their name, their reputation, their dignity, their place in society, their place in history, what people think of them!). What is important are the experiments they are performing, the completion of their work—that seventh volume on the snail! The ability of scientists to be so utterly dedicated to their work is most admirable; one praises God for having given people such wonderful power. But one also stops to think: at what cost? The danger is that it be at the cost of themselves. When this is the case, then this admirable self-giving becomes tragic self-losing.

A "Christian" critique of the university is concerned with this fourfold temptation of the scientist—pride, pretending to know what he does not know, naturalism and self-forgetting —because Jesus Christ judges the scientist on the basis of these temptations even more than on the excellence of his scientific achievements.

IV

8. The doctrine of evolution permeates university existence at every level. It is taken for granted as an indisputable fact, almost as divine revelation. In the atmosphere of the university you inhale it as the air you breathe. To question its validity is almost to cause one to appear a fool. It purports to explain every-

thing: beauty, goodness, malice, mind, honesty, holiness; or if it does not bother to explain them, it dismisses them as "relative" and unimportant. These things "evolved," and that settles the matter. Let any fundamental question arise and forthwith the mind jumps, as to a *deus ex machina*, to the doctrine of evolution for the rescue. It has almost replaced truth as the first principle of the university: it is itself the truth.

Since university existence is wholly identified with this doctrine, even to hint at the possibility of questioning it or limiting the scope of its validity has the effect of placing one outside the pale of the university altogether. A doubter of this doctrine simply does not belong to the university: he is ruled out. I mean a real doubter, not one who doubts it in private but would not dare raise his voice against it with his colleagues.

Therefore, a Christian critique of the university must confront this situation with the utmost sense of responsibility and with total scientific competence. Such a critique would marshal three arguments from different orders of being:

(a) From the strict scientific evidence—is the objective, scientific evidence as compelling as the votaries of the doctrine claim? Or may their original, existential, a priori predilection for the doctrine (a predilection that anteceded the evidence and had something to do with it and did in fact determine the search for and the selection of the evidence) itself not have compelled them to the doctrine? The strictest scientific integrity should govern this argument.

(b) From the fateful confusion between idea and fact, between theory and phenomenon (in the phenomenological sense of the term). The "truth" of evolution is the truth of an idea, a theory, an inference, and not the truth of immediately given phenomena, such as the fact that we are limited, we are fallible, we are mortal, we are vain, we gossip, we scheme, we love, we hate, we are lonely, we are anxious, we get embarrassed and then act in funny ways, we often make fools of ourselves, we are miserable when our rivals best us.

Therefore, the evaluation of the truth of the theory of evolution awaits the working out of the truth of any theory in contradistinction to the truth of immediate phenomena. The Christian can say to the evolutionist: your theory is cogent and beautiful; it has impressed me no end; but it is a theory all the same; it is not an immediate phenomenon reflecting existence, being; and, my friend, it is not theories, no matter how beautiful and "true," but such phenomena that matter most in your life and mine, including the life of the theorizing mind itself.

(c) From the original, irreducible, spiritual nature of human beings. By this I mean asking the evolutionist really to make an effort to acquaint himself firsthand with authentic religious existence. This entails knowing, really and personally, the life of the church in all its richness including its wonderful variegated liturgy; reading the Bible again and again, especially the Psalms and the New Testament; contemplating the great religious art in Rome, Paris and Madrid, and wherever it is to be found in palaces and museums; visiting, spending some time at and studying the great cathedrals, including Agia Sophia of Constantinople; soaking oneself in sacred music, both Western and Eastern; contemplating Byzantine, and especially Russian, iconography; reading the lives and writings of some twenty great saints; absorbing, as much as possible, the metaphysical poetry of the seventeenth century; and living for some time in an existing rooted Christian community. There is no truth without gathering in all the evidence, and authentic religious existence in all its modes and forms throughout the ages belongs to the total evidence about the nature of man. It purports to be dealing with nothing else. It unconceals a side of human nature (creatureliness, adoration, love, community, self-overcoming, self-giving, self-forgetting, hope, trust) that no other side dreams of. A man really seeking, seriously seeking, honestly seeking to understand the nature of man, I mean the seeker's own nature including even his biological origin, cannot, without being "unscientific," limit himself to the study of fossils, of primitive forms of life, both human and subhuman, and of comparative morphology and physiology. Shouldn't actual living-dying human existence itself be sought and consulted? When an evolutionist, or any human being, liberates himself from the cage of his professional deformation and personally seeks and discovers the religious evidence, he is likely to see awakened in himself a certain "original, irreducible, spiritual nature" which was there all the time, dormant, concealed and covered up, awaiting unconcealment and release. He will then laugh at any theory, "scientific" or otherwise, whose effect would be either to deny the existence of this "spiritual nature" which he has discovered in himself, or, which amounts to the same thing, to derive it from something other than itself or from nothing.

When the theory of evolution is adequately confronted with these three orders of being it will take its rightful place in the scheme of things, a place that turns out to be not very interesting, and in any event very subsidiary. The philosophical, moral, human, spiritual and ontological consequences that have been erected on the base of the doctrine of evolution will then all crumble.

V

The "creationists" missed the whole point in their dispute with the evolutionists in a trial at a court in Little Rock, Arkansas, recently. They argued that there is such a thing as "creation science." The truth is that there is no such thing. They cannot "scientifically prove" that God created the world, including man, according to the biblical account, whether in Genesis or elsewhere. The word *science* means something very precise today. According to this meaning the sciences are one thing, the Bible is something else altogether.

Science operates according to special procedures (observation, experimentation, verification, precise description, measurement, public scrutiny by experts, world recognition and acceptance, etc.) which have been progressively refined since Pythagoras, Hippocrates and Archimedes. Science is what takes place in the laboratories and departments of science in the great universities and technical institutes, and in the great industrial and defense establishments, and certainly the Bible is not part of what takes place there.

Science has acquired such overpowering prestige today that, according to some people, you cannot hope to get a hearing for what you are talking about unless it is science. Therefore, conclude the "creationists," let us show that we too are scientists! This attitude is called scientism: the worship of science as understood today as the only or the highest avenue to the truth. What if there are things in life (life itself, love, freedom, tragedy, decision, fellowship, friendship, community, loneliness, rebellion, suffering, resentment, ambition, hope, hopelessness, death) which have nothing to do with science? And what if these things are more important than anything that science deals with? Insofar as the scientist knows these things and experiences them in his own life, he does not draw them *out of* his science: he already brings them with him *to* his science. Thus to want to show that the Bible is *also* science is not to understand either the nature of science or the dignity of the Bible. It is to demean the Bible rather than to exalt it. It is in effect to look upon science as superior and to subordinate the Bible to science. The exact opposite is the truth if the two are to be compared at all: the Bible and what it means and stands for is superior, and science and what it means, asserts and delivers is subordinate.

Science is the product of the community of the scientists, the Bible the product of the community of the faithful as inspired by God. Neither is the creation of individuals in isolation; both are expressions of the life and activity of rooted communities. The spirit, the principle, of the community of faith, which is the church, is love and self-sacrifice, and this is not the spirit of the community of science. The scientists are not noted for loving or sacrificing to one another, and if they do so they bring the spirit of love and sacrifice from outside their science. They are more celebrated for their rivalries and jealousies, and for making sure that their ideas and discoveries are not plagiarized by others but are exclusively attributed to them while some of them do not mind plagiarizing others themselves. They, their name and their authorship rights are uppermost on their mind. If we are to characterize the spirit of the scientific community we will have to say that in the final analysis it is passion for knowledge with a view to power. Scientists want to control and dominate their material and through it, if possible, the world, both the material world and the human world. Science is an expression of the will to power.

In the community of love, the church, it is not a question of power and control; it is not even a question of knowledge in the scientific sense of the term. It is exclusively a question of remembering and loving, in a communal celebration or act, him who loved us and gave his life for us, even Jesus Christ of Nazareth. Those who do not know him and his love do not belong to the community and cannot be expected to share our faith. "For whosoever shall call upon the name of the Lord shall be saved. How then shall they call on him in whom they have not believed? and how shall they believe in him of whom they have not heard? and how shall they hear without a preacher? And how shall they preach, except they be sent?"[5] Faith in God the Creator of heaven and earth and of everything visible and invisible is the natural expression of a living order of love, grounded in Jesus Christ, both historically and ontologically, and not of any scientific ratiocination. If we live our faith—taking part in all the feasts and occasions of worship of the church, rejoicing in the Lord with the community, reading the Bible regularly, repenting for our sins and infirmities, bearing part of the burden of the church, fulfilling our church obligations, accepting suffering for the sake of the community of faith, witnessing to Christ in life and word, educating ourselves in the literature of the church, really interesting ourselves in what is happening today to the Christian communities all over the world, following the movement of evangelization all over the world, steeping ourselves in the great sacred literature, art and music, leisurely meditating with friends in the Holy Spirit on the mystery of the life of the spirit, thinking of Jesus Christ all the time and loving him above everything in the world including ourselves, always giving God the praise and glory—then faith in God the Creator of everything from nothing is the most natural and unshakable thing we acquire, and we neither ask nor care to ask for any certification of this faith from any science. "All things are delivered to me of my Father: and no man knoweth who the Son is, but the Father; and who the Father is, but the Son, and he to whom the Son will reveal him."[6]

Therefore, instead of the "creationists" worrying how to prove that they too are "scientists," which they cannot prove, they should worry about why they cannot produce a single Nobel Prize winner in medicine or physics or chemistry or biology or any of the sciences, who is at the same time a firm and outspoken believer in the crucified and resurrected Jesus whose glory is that he is now and forever at the very right hand of God, and who therefore is Lord of lords and King of kings, and the savior of himself and the only real hope of the world. They simply cannot produce such a man because such a man does not exist: I mean a man who is recognized and quoted by the scientific communities all over the world (in Tokyo, Peking, Delhi, Moscow, Freiburg, the Sorbonne, Oxford, Harvard) as a world authority in his own field, whose contributions are organically incorporated in world science everywhere just as, for instance, the contributions of Maxwell or Einstein or Planck or Fermi are recognized and made use of by the scientific communities all over the world, and who at the same time will stand up in public and recite the Nicene Creed and declare that he believes every word of it, as an expression of the community of love to which he belongs, I mean the church, exactly as Athanasius and the Council of Nicea meant it in the year 325 and as the church has affirmed and taught it since. He need not be a Nobel Prize winner, but he must be a recognized world authority; neither need he go to the court in Little Rock, Arkansas, to deposit his testimony: he can write it in rigorous fashion, setting forth both his scientific credentials and his personal witness to his Christian faith, and then publish it in *Time* magazine or *The New York Times* or *Science* (the organ of The American Association for the Advancement of Science). It is such a public deposition by such a man that will produce the greatest wholesome shock possible in both the scientific and the religious communities, serving the interests of both of them: the interests of the scientists by humbling them with the objective-existential proof that faith in creation is not incompatible with whatever "truth" the theory of evolution might hold, and the interests of the religious community by liberating it from any worry lest "science" contradict the most orthodox expression of the Christian faith. I repeat, the "creationists" must produce such a man, and that is their real problem.

There are great medical doctors who sincerely believe, but I doubt that any of them owes his faith to his science. They acquired it from outside their science altogether—from the order of love and grace in which they were brought up. They imported it with them into their science. And their science did not destroy it in them because medicine is much more than science. Medicine as a profession deals with suffering, anxious, living-dying humanity, and the doctor himself belongs to this very humanity, and therefore knows very well what suffering, anxiety, and life and death mean.

Now love and grace sprout nowhere save in the very being of the soil of living-dying humanity. And so if the doctor brings his faith with him to the practice of his profession he is likely to retain it. And even the doctors who come from atheistic or neutral backgrounds will sooner or later acquire a certain wholesome wistfulness about the ultimate issues of life and death and suffering. This wistfulness can never by itself yield faith in God; it may only cause the wistful doctor to search for God, even if he is not aware that he is searching for him or does not know how to search for him; and if he should find him he would find him neither in science nor in medicine but only where he is and where he authentically declares himself, to wit, in the living order of grace and love. The question, however, remains: Is the believing doctor still in such an existential-moral position as to be able to say the Creed in total honesty and with an absolutely clear conscience?

The man the creationists must produce does not exist, and this is what they should worry about, this is what they should anxiously inquire into. He does not exist either (a) because the scientific community, for reasons of its own, does not accept, whether by set policy or by subtle discouragement, real Christian believers to join its fellowship but only non-Christians; or (b) because scientists, coming from homes, backgrounds and traditions of authentic Christian faith, soon lose their faith's hold on them and take on, by the natural workings of laws of social assimilation, the preponderant naturalist-immanentist-agnostic-atheistic-secularist color of the general scientific community with which they live and interact; or (c) because, whether or not they are originally excluded or discouraged, and whether or not their original vibrant faith withers away by sheer social and professional contamination, there is essential incompatibility between worshiping and loving Jesus Christ and dedicating oneself to the pursuit of science.

I doubt (a) and (c) and am inclined to pin the cause on (b). If (a) is the reason (and I see no evidence of the scientific community discriminating against believing Christians provided they really excel in their science), we are dealing with an accidental phenomenon which can be exposed and remedied. If (c) is the reason, then we are in the presence of a most serious situation: Christ hates our investigating and knowing the truths which science explores and discovers, and we are to choose between Christ, letting go scientific knowledge, or scientific knowledge, letting go Christ. I do not believe the Eternal Logos, who is Jesus Christ himself, "in whom are hid all the treasures of wisdom and knowledge,"[7] is essentially opposed to the knowledge of any truth whatever it be and however it be arrived at. This does not exclude the possibility, due to our natural infirmities, of getting so fascinated ourselves by our human knowledge as to bow down before it and worship it and therefore worship ourselves. Only the compassionate God, who constantly reminds us of and brings us back to himself, can safeguard us against this Satanic pitfall. If we are thus reduced to alternative (b) then the question arises: Why has the naturalist-immanentist-atheistic-secularist bent of mind preponderated in the scientific community to the extent that the radical Judaeo-Christian-Islamic transcendentalism can no longer be maintained in that community?

A couple of years ago a Muslim Pakistani won a Nobel Award in physics. Many other people were also honored with Nobel Prizes for their diverse accomplishments. The press interviewed most of them about their reactions to the awards when they first heard of them. With the exception of the Pakistani, they all said that they were overjoyed, that they celebrated with their families and friends, and they expressed the normal feelings of satisfaction that people experience on such occasions. Only the Pakistani said that his first act was to pray to Allah (God) and thank him for having illuminated his mind and enabled it to penetrate some of the mysteries of his creation. Knowing Islamic piety, I am sure the Pakistani scientist was most truthful and sincere. I do not know the religion of the other recipients of the Nobel Awards, nor indeed whether any of them belongs to any religion, but none of them, it seems, so much as thought of God. One of the many admirable characteristics of Islam is its absolute faith in the transcendent "Creator of the heavens and the earth and all that is between them," who is exalted above every thought or description. And the Muslim scientist first thought of Allah (God) and not of himself or of science or of truth or of nature or of his own achievement. The Christian scientists, if a scientist could still be or remain Christian, can emulate the Muslims in their total fidelity to their faith and in the courage with which they confess it from the housetops.

Christian believers who call themselves "creationists" (a term which simply signifies what I have just called "the radical Judaeo-Christian-Islamic transcendentalism") must inquire into and ponder these questions. They should set about producing great scientists who receive Nobel Prizes and still recite the Credo and sincerely and unstammeringly believe every word of it. When they really start thinking seriously of these matters, they will inevitably find themselves embarking on a Christian critique of the university like the one we are attempting here. For the university these days is the fountainhead at once of truth and of deviation from the truth.

VI

9. The ultimate, basic presupposition of present-day science is that the universe is self-creative. Matter is always there to begin with and life somehow "evolved" from matter. As to mind, this too is wholly determined by life and matter, and somehow "evolved" from them. The processes and phenomena of mind, life and matter are wholly self-enclosed, self-sufficient and self-explanatory. To look beyond and outside them in any sense of "beyond" and "outside," even with the strict intention of not impairing their relative autonomy and freedom in the slightest, is sheer obscurantism if not lunacy. Thus the question of sources and origins must be radically raised and vigorously sustained in the face of this unabashed monism which causes everything in the end to collapse onto the drabness of the one uniform plane of matter. How the infinite qualitative multiplicity of actual, given existence ever arose from this unrelieved drabness and uniformity is a miracle. The antecedent determination of will is this: stubbornly to maintain the monistic principle at all costs, even if that should land one in faith in miracles.

No moment could have been more serious or solemn for Socrates in all his life than when he was conversing with his friends in prison just before he drank the hemlock. He said that in his youth he was fond of natural science and the way it explained the coming to being and the perishing of things. It did not take him long to feel that this naturalistic method of explanation was unsatisfactory:

"When I was young, Cebes, I had a remarkable enthusiasm for the kind of wisdom known as natural science; it seemed to me magnificent to know the causes of everything, why a thing comes into being, why it perishes, why it exists. Often I used to shift backwards and forwards trying to answer questions like this, to start with: Is it when the conjunction of the hot and the cold results in putrefaction that living creatures develop? Is it blood that we think with, or air or fire? Or is thought due to something else, namely the brain's providing our senses of hearing, sight and smell, which give rise to memory and judgement, and ultimately, when memory and judgement have acquired stability, to knowledge?

"Next I tried to investigate how things perish, and what went on in the heavens and on the earth, until in the end I decided that I had simply no gift whatever for this sort of investigation. To show how right I was about that, I may tell you that, whereas there were some things which up till then I had, as I thought myself and other people thought too, definitely understood, I was now smitten with such complete blindness as the result of my investigations that I unlearnt even what I previously thought I knew, including more particularly the cause of a human being's growth. I had supposed that to be obvious to anybody: he grew because he ate and drank; on taking food flesh was added to flesh, bone to bone, and similarly the appropriate matter was added to each part of a man, until in the end his small bulk had become a large one, and so the little child had become a big man. That was what I used to believe: reasonably enough, wouldn't you say?...

"One day, however, I heard someone reading an extract

from what he said was a book by Anaxagoras, to the effect that it is Mind [Nous] that arranges all things in order and causes all things; now there was a cause that delighted me, for I felt that in a way it was good that Mind should be the cause of everything; and I decided that if this were true Mind must do all its ordering and arranging in the fashion that is best for each individual thing. Hence if one wanted to discover the cause for anything coming into being or perishing or existing, the question to ask was how it was best for that thing to exist or to act or be acted upon. On this principle then the only thing that a man had to think about, whether in regard to himself or anything else, was what is best, what is the highest good; though of course he would also have to know what is bad, since knowledge of good involves knowledge of bad. With these reflexions I was delighted to think I had found in Anaxagoras an instructor about the cause of things after my own heart; I expected him to tell me in the first place whether the earth is flat or round, and then go on to explain the cause why it must be the one or the other, using the term "better", and showing how it was better for it to be as it is; and then if he said the earth is in the centre of the universe, he would proceed to explain how it was better for it to be there. If he could make all these things plain to me, I was ready to abandon the quest of any other sort of cause. Indeed I was ready to go further, applying the same principle of inquiry to sun, moon and stars, their relative velocities and turnings and so forth: I would ask which is the better way for these bodies to act or be acted upon. For I never supposed that when Anaxagoras had said that they are ordered by Mind he would bring in some other cause for them, and not be content with showing that it is best for them to be as they are; I imagined that in assigning the cause of particular things and of things in general he would proceed to explain what was the individual best and the general good; and I wouldn't have sold my hopes for a fortune. I made all haste to get hold of the books, and read them as soon as ever I could, in order to discover without delay what was best and what was worst.

"And then, my friend, from my marvellous height of hope I came hurtling down; for as I went on with my reading I found the man making no use of Mind, not crediting it with any causality for setting things in order, but finding causes in things like air and aether and water and a host of other absurdities. It seemed to me that his position was like that of a man who said that all the actions of Socrates are due to his mind, and then attempted to give the causes of my several actions by saying that the reason why I am now sitting here is that my body is composed of bones and sinews, and the bones are hard and separated by joints, while the sinews, which can be tightened or relaxed, envelop the bones along with the flesh and skin which hold them together; so that when the bones move about in their sockets, the sinews, by lessening or increasing the tension, make it possible for me at this moment to bend my limbs, and that is the cause of my sitting here in this bent position. Analogous causes might also be given of my conversing with you, sounds, air-currents, streams of hearing and so on and so forth, to the neglect of the true causes, to wit that, inasmuch as the Athenians have thought it better to condemn me, I too in my turn think it better to sit here, and more right and proper to stay where I am and submit to such punishment as they enjoin. For, by Jingo, I fancy these same sinews and bones would long since have been somewhere in Megara or Boeotia, impelled by their notion of what was best, if I had not thought it right and proper to submit to the penalty appointed by the State rather than take to my heels and run away.

"No: to call things like that causes is quite absurd; it would be true to say that if I did not possess things like that—bones and sinews and so on—I shouldn't be able to do what I had resolved upon; but to say that I do what I do because of them— and that too when I am acting with my mind—and not be-cause of my choice of what is best, would be to use extremely careless language. Fancy not being able to distinguish be-tween the cause of a thing and that without which the cause would not be a cause! It is evidently this latter that most peo-ple, groping in the dark, call by the name of cause, a name which doesn't belong to it. . . ."

Then Socrates goes on to posit the Ideas or Forms which con-stitute the essence of Platonism, namely, that there is Beauty in itself, Justice in itself, Goodness in itself, "and so on with the rest of them."

"Now consider whether you think as I do about the next point. It appears to me that if anything else is beautiful be-sides the beautiful itself the sole reason for its being so is that it participates in that beautiful; and I assert that the same principle applies in all cases. . . .

"It follows that I can no longer understand nor recognise those other learned causes which they speak of; if anyone tells me that the reason why such-and-such a thing is beauti-ful is that it has a bright colour or a certain shape or something of that kind, I take no notice of it all, for I find it all confusing, save for one fact, which in my simple, naive and maybe fool-ish fashion I hug close: namely that what makes a thing beau-tiful is nothing other than the presence or communion of that beautiful itself . . . [I] merely affirm that all beautiful things are beautiful because of the beautiful itself. That seems to me the safest answer for me to give whether to myself or to another; if I hold fast to that I feel I am not likely to come to grief; yes, the safe course is to tell myself or anybody else that beautiful things are beautiful because of the beautiful itself."[8]

VII

Groping for the living God.

Considering the existential circumstances under which it was said, and who said it, and who recorded the saying for all time, what Socrates is saying here is probably the noblest intellectual cry that has come down to us from the heathen world.

Nothing closer to God then than this cry.

There is unutterable, hidden suffering underneath.

Total disenchantment with this world.

The heart craves, demands, cries for the unchangeableness of eternity.

There must be "somewhere" Beauty in itself, Goodness in itself, Justice in itself.

All worldly beauties, goodnesses, justices are nonsense without *the* beautiful, *the* good, *the* just.

Elements by themselves, whatever combinations and permutations they may assume, and matter by itself, whatever complexity or configuration it may take, can never give rise to beauty, justice, goodness, life, mind, spirit.

There must be original and separate Life, Justice, Mind for this living thing, this just person, this thinking mind to exist.

Otherwise magic, superstition, witchcraft; otherwise something from nothing.

Ye atheistic evolutionists, hear!

How close the heart of Socrates and Plato to the living God —almost there!

But still alas in idea.

Still rationally, intellectually.

Still in deadly loneliness.

Still far from living love.

"I have heard of thee by the hearing of the ear: but now mine eye seeth thee. Wherefore I abhor myself, and repent in dust and ashes."[9]

This Socrates could not say; this, unknowingly, how much in his heart of hearts he wanted to be able to say!

"When thou saidst, Seek ye my face; my heart said unto thee, Thy face, LORD, will I seek. Hide not thy face far from me."[10]

This Socrates could not say; this, unknowingly, how much in his heart of hearts he wanted to be able to say!

"Lord, what wilt thou have me to do?"[11]

This Socrates could not say; this, unknowingly, how much in his heart of hearts he was dying to be able to say!

Socrates and Plato had no notion of the Thou whom they could thus personally address on their knees, as Job, David and Paul did.

"In the beginning was the Word, and the Word was with God, and the Word was God. . . . In him was life; . . . And the Word was made flesh, and dwelt among us, (and we beheld his glory, the glory as of the only begotten of the Father,) full of grace and truth. . . . For the law [Idea] was given by Moses, but grace and truth came by Jesus Christ."[12]

This Socrates never heard and could not understand because he did not "behold his glory," not even in the mode of expectation which was granted to David; this, unknowingly, how much in his heart of hearts Socrates was dying all his life to hear and understand!

"I am the resurrection, and the life: he that believeth in me, though he were dead, yet shall he live: And whosoever liveth and believeth in me shall never die."[13]

This Socrates never heard, but had he been with Martha and

Mary then he would have perfectly understood it, far better than Martha and Mary did; this, unknowingly, how much in his heart of hearts Socrates was dying all his life to hear precisely from him who said it, in order to understand and believe!

"Blessed are the pure in heart: for they shall see God."[14]

The incredibly pure heart of Socrates entitled him to see God.

With the knowledge of faith, I know he shall see God.

I used the word "unknowingly" five times above.

Realizing perfectly, in their unbelievable genius, this failing of theirs, the Greeks set up an altar "To The Unknown God,"[15] signifying that while in their polytheism they had erected altars to every conceivable god, they still might have missed one.

"Whom therefore ye ignorantly worship," said Paul to the Athenians, "him declare I unto you";[16] and he confronted them with the one and only true God who gave "assurance unto all men" about the "man whom he hath ordained" by raising "him from the dead."[17]

Today in Greece there is not a single altar to any pagan god, and yet the country is full of churches dedicated to the very man whom God hath ordained, whom he raised "from the dead," and many of these churches are named after that very Paul whom the pagan Athenians called a "babbler."[18]

Even Plato was dissatisfied with the Idea, dead and all by itself. In the *Sophist* he cried for life.

"Stranger. But tell me, in heaven's name: are we really to be so easily convinced that change, life, soul, understanding have no place in that which is perfectly real [the Idea, the Form]—that it has neither life nor thought, but stands immutable in solemn aloofness, devoid of intelligence?

Theaetetus. That, sir, would be a strange doctrine to accept.

Stranger. But can we say it has intelligence without having life?

Theaetetus. Surely not.

Stranger. But if we say it contains both, can we deny that it has soul in which they reside?

Theaetetus. How else could it possess them?"[19]

It is life, life, real life, authentic life, eternal life, that all philosophy ultimately seeks.

How much Socrates, Plato and Aristotle would have rejoiced in hearing with their own ears and seeing him who said it with their own eyes: "I am the way, the truth, and the life"![20]

They would have rejoiced, and believed.

VIII

The basic number is two and not one. The most fundamental distinction is between creature and Creator; and not just any "creator" such as Plato's *Demiurgos* or even Aristotle's God, but a *Creator from nothing, (ex nihilo)*, namely, a Creator who is "wholly other." All other distinctions are secondary to this one. Where this distinction is blurred, where the absolute twoness of God and man is replaced by the bland oneness of "the universe," confusion, and worse than confusion, reigns. Monism disguises human arrogance and pride. The oneness of monism is but a projection onto "the universe" of the self-sufficiency of man. The comfortable safety of monism is a pitiable illusion.

O proud man, whom takest thou thyself to be? Thou art mortal. Thou art fearful of death every minute. How can therefore thy views of God, thyself and "the universe" be taken seriously? How can they be trusted? Thou seethest with innumerable infirmities and defects. Thou hidest them underneath the cloak of thy self-sufficiency. How false, how pitiful a self-sufficiency when thou art mortal, fallible, perilously treading on the thinnest ice every moment of thy life! "We spend our years as a tale that is told. The days of our years are threescore years and ten;

and if by reason of strength they be fourscore years, yet is their strength labour and sorrow; for it is soon cut off, and we fly away."[21] Dost thou not see that "our iniquities," "our secret sins" are there, no matter how much thou dissemblest them? Dost thou not know that Someone hath set them before him, and keepeth them in the light of his countenance, all the time?[22]

Knowing all this about thee, this same Someone loveth thee all the same and hath given his life for thee to the end that thou be born again, this time his brother and a son of God.[23] Thou canst not go from his spirit, thou canst not flee from his presence.[24] If only thou knew, if only thou confessed, if only thou repented! But thou wilt never be able to do that until he meet thee face to face and thou fall on thy knees before him.

O proud man, wilt thou ever fall on thy knees? Thou shalt remain the slave of thy pride until then. But when the appointed time to be liberated cometh, thou wilt be reborn a free man, a true man, for the first time. "I have heard of thee by the hearing of the ear: but now mine eye seeth thee. Wherefore I abhor myself, and repent in dust and ashes."[25] And how much thou then shalt shed joyful tears, and how much thou shalt laugh! And how much thy science will be perfected, and will glorify him who liberated thee!

Scientists are for the most part naturalists. They worship nature. These processes that they investigate, together with their thought about them, are all that there is. They think they are quite happy in resting in them. Are they as happy as they think? They have been seduced by nature; they thus forget themselves. What about their personal problems—problems of aging and death and disease and anxiety and loneliness and scheming and resentment and spite and despair and frustrated ambition and that utter tastelessness and disgust and meaninglessness of existence which sometimes seize them? They do not want to be reminded of these things; but they are there all the time. What have their experiments and investigations to do with these things? What about even worse things that befall them?

Let scientists then open-mindedly and without a priori bias and rejection read the first chapter of Saint Paul's Epistle to the Romans. They should read it every day. For there is no more effective spiritual therapy they can undergo than seriously pondering this chapter. Some will not so much as touch this book because they think it will pollute them. But let those who are gifted with the true scientific attitude of being able to rise above their built-in antecedent horror and prejudice, let them humbly and self-examiningly read this chapter. "That which may be known of God" by reason and nature "is manifest in them; for God hath shewed it unto them. For the invisible things of him from the creation of the world are clearly seen, being understood by the things that are made, even his eternal power and God-head; so that, "if they do not acknowledge this and draw the proper consequences therefrom, then "they are without excuse." God forbid that this should happen to them; God forbid that they do not "glorify him as God," that they be not "thankful," that they "become vain in their imaginations," that "their foolish heart become darkened," that they change "the glory of the uncorruptible God into an image made like to corruptible man, and to birds, and fourfooted beasts, and creeping things." Because then God will give them up "to uncleanness through the lusts of their own hearts." If they change "the truth of God into a lie," if they worship and serve "the creature more than the Creator, who is blessed for ever," then God will give them up "unto vile affections." This "giving them up," this giving them over "to a reprobate mind," is an inevitable consequence of turning one's back on the Creator and one's face to the creature.

Let the scientists examine themselves closely and make sure

that none of the twenty-four misfortunes enumerated at the end of the chapter has overtaken them. God loves them and fully approves of their search for the truth of the creature. God does not want them to perish at all. If the scientist forgoes his existential loneliness and loses himself in the fellowship of the church (this is impossible without existential humility), he can still earn the Nobel Prize for some breakthrough into the atom without losing his hold on God, or, more precisely, without God letting go his hold upon him.

IX

10. A Christian critique of the university aims at ascertaining, in fear and trembling, what Jesus Christ thinks of the university. Science in this age plays a dominant role in the overall life of the university. Can Jesus Christ, the Eternal Logos, he "in whom are hid all the treasures of wisdom and knowledge," he who is the only real lover of mankind, including of course the scientist, can he be indifferent to any truth, which in itself and within its proper limits is sacred, arrogating to itself a status and an order not its own; to the confusion and helplessness which invariably assail the poor scientist when he finds himself lost amidst the boundless proliferation of knowledge in his own field which he can neither compass nor wholly keep up with; to the great difficulty of bringing progress in any one science (or the wisdom one accumulates from life's "nonscientific experience at large"), in time and at the rate at which that progress occurs, to bear critically and creatively upon progress in the other sciences; to the frightfully accelerating multiplication of knowledge these days, a multiplication which resists, because of the inherent limitations of the human mind, being ordered into a coherent whole, even by the two disciplines, philosophy and theology, which are by nature ordained precisely to that end; to the illicit

transfer of what is called today "the scientific method" to realms altogether outside the province of "the sciences" to which that method properly applies; to the moral and "scientific" confusion which results from the scientists not being scientific enough to refrain from pronouncing on matters (e.g., God, freedom and destiny) in which they, as scientists, are wholly incompetent; to the scientists today almost invariably falling into pride of knowledge, pretense of knowledge, worship of nature (naturalism, pantheism, atheism) and hypocritical self-forgetfulness in which they are simply fleeing from themselves; to the moral, intellectual, spiritual and existential havoc wrought in the fields of morality, religion, culture, philosophy (especially epistemology and ontology), the interpretation of history, and even cosmology, from the manifold false and unwarranted conclusions drawn from the theory of evolution; and to the tendency of science to foster in the scientist the deadly sense of human self-sufficiency, disguising itself in radical immanentism, naturalistic monism and the doctrine of the self-creativity of "the universe," and issuing in unabashed atheism and the denial of God, Christ and the Holy Spirit? Can Jesus Christ ignore all this? He cannot.

CHAPTER FIVE

———

THE HUMANITIES

THE SCIENCES ARE IMPORTANT so far as a Christian critique of the university is concerned, but the humanities are even more important; and if the humanities were themselves in a healthy state, from the point of view of Jesus Christ, they would provide the right and necessary corrective to the problems of the sciences.

For the purposes of this investigation, by the humanities I mean history, literature, philosophy, psychology, art, religion, sociology, politics, economics and the study of other cultures. There are clear distinctions to be made between these ten departments (for instance, between the so-called social sciences and the strictly intellectual and spiritual disciplines), but these distinctions do not affect the main thrust of my argument. Also the fact that each one of these departments breaks up within itself into several subdepartments (for instance, philosophy into logic, aesthetics, epistemology, ethics, etc.; history into national history, Western history, world history, etc.; literature into national literature and comparative literature; art into architecture, sculpture, painting, music, etc.; etc.), while very important even for our purposes, can be abstracted from without impairing our general argument.

I

The fundamental spirit of the whole university is determined by the humanities. Philosophically and spiritually, where the humanities stand, the entire university stands—administrators, professors and students, individually and, what is more determinant, in their meetings in groups. The view of the nature and destiny of man, the general outlook on life and being, the interpretation of history, the fundamental orientation of the mind, the formation of personal character and the fixing of basic attitudes and habits, the nature of good and bad and right and wrong, the meaning and purpose of human existence, the whole spirit which stamps the individual human person—all these radiate in the first instance, not from the sciences, but from what is taught and presupposed in the humanities. And the example of the life of the teacher is here most decisive. I say "presupposed," because what is presupposed is often far more subtle and potent than what is explicitly taught; what you are silent about will pass as something so much taken for granted that you do not need to say a word about it; while what you explicitly put forward may be arguable. Therefore seek first what the university is silent about, and then you know the secret of the university. The scientist himself, both when he takes courses in general education as an undergraduate student and from the general climate of opinion of the university, is stamped in his mind and character by the pervasive spirit of the university, whatever that be, which, as we saw, is originally determined by the humanities.

Is it fair to lump all the humanities in one basket? So far as the diversity of their material contents is concerned, it is not fair; but so far as the virtual identity of the element missing in all of them is concerned, it is eminently fair. Certainly the subject matter of history is one thing, and the subject matter of literature is another; certainly the subject matter of sociology is one thing, and the subject matter of philosophy is another. But there is something almost universally absent in all the humanities, and that is any reference to something genuinely transcendent: the number one, and not the number two, is basic to them, just as it is to the sciences.

But how can this be when we include religion among the humanities? Is not the first principle of religion the ultimacy of the transcendent principle, the radical distinction between creature and Creator? This is certainly the first principle of religion, but is it maintained in the departments of religion in the universities?

Again I remind the reader that this is not an intellectual or a humanist critique of the university; it is not even a "general religious" critique: it is a "Christian" critique. Our guiding question is, What does Jesus Christ himself think of the university? The mind is at once and throughout set on Christ.

The general secularizing of the university has invaded and seized the universities' departments of religion. These departments are vying with one another as to how to make their deliveries "relevant" and acceptable to the present age. The demands of "relevance" preoccupy their mind. Can you imagine the department of religion in any one of the fifty greatest universities in the Western world teaching the Holy Trinity, the Incarnation, the resurrection, etc., in such a way that the intent of the teaching would be acceptable to Augustine, Chrysostom, Damascenus, Basil the Great and Thomas Aquinas? Saint Paul would not recognize himself in them; they hardly even

71

respect his original intent, let alone believe in it; they must always "interpret" him to suit the mind of the age, the times, the *saecularis*; far from trying to transform the *saecularis* to conform to his original intent, they go to great pains to transform him, and in the process to distort him altogether, so as to conform to the vagaries of the *saecularis*.[1] And as to Jesus Christ, certainly he will enter everywhere, even into the departments of religion of the universities, because he loves everybody, especially the searching, and the straying and lost, and indeed the straying and lost even more than the searching. "Whither shall I go from thy spirit? or whither shall I flee from thy presence? If I ascend up into heaven, thou art there: if I make my bed in hell, behold, thou art there. If I take the wings of the morning, and dwell in the uttermost parts of the sea; Even there shall thy hand lead me, and thy right hand shall hold me. If I say, Surely the darkness shall cover me; even the night shall be light about me. Yea, the darkness hideth not from thee; but the night shineth as the day: the darkness and the light are both alike to thee."[2]

No, Jesus Christ will enter everywhere; he will enter even the departments of religion of the universities, which have gone the way of all flesh in becoming secularized like other departments of the humanities—in departing from doctrinal communion with the Fathers and Saints in order to achieve communion with the *saecularis*. But having entered these halls, how long will he stay in them? Having entered them, mustn't people then, in their original God-given freedom, take the initiative of making some kind of response?

We should now be more precise. What is the "spirit" that pervades the humanities today? What does Jesus Christ himself think of this "spirit"? This is exactly our task. We spoke of genuine transcendence, we adverted to secularism and the *saecularis*, we referred to the numbers two and one. Let us try now, in a very provisional manner, to fill these formalities with matter and content.

II

The spirit, the fundamental presupposition, of the humanities today is characterized by the following:

1. *Naturalism.* Nature is all in all; therefore the worship of nature. This is principally the outcome of the impact of science, but it is also a reversion to ancient heathenism. Moreover the heathenism of Asia and Africa is making inroads into the spirit of the West.

2. *Subjectivism.* The subject, the ego, is the first principle; everything is to be excogitated, attested, by it. Nothing can surprise the subject from outside. The "I," "das Ich," reigns. Ultimately this goes back to the rebellion of the modern age against the objective realism of the medieval period. In modern times Descartes and German Idealism are its fountainhead.

3. *Rationalism.* What is meant here is not the possession or use of reason, because everybody, in every age and under every circumstance, uses reason; and without reason man ceases to be man. What is meant is the belief that reason is all-sufficient and therefore can explain everything; and not only that, but it is all-powerful and can bring about everything. Rationalism is the ancient Greek fallacy which asserts that knowledge is virtue: once you know the good, then you will automatically go ahead and do it. Rationalism is the rationalist expression of subjectivism; therefore it is a narrowing down of subjectivism, which allows also for passion and will.

4. *Skepticism.* Nothing certain. No absolute. All ultimately misty. Living in a world of doubt and suspicion. Every sentence hedged by some reservation, some warning, some caveat. Oh,

yes, tomes and tomes of argument and discussion—very ingenious, very brilliant, very entertaining; but you ask yourself at the end, What does the whole exercise come to? Literally nothing, since everything changes. "Times change" is always the answer and excuse. Consider how much Hume was impressed by the chaotic stream of impressions. And Hume's influence on Anglo-Saxon thought is considerable. Consider, too, in this connection Whitehead's definition of the self as "a personal society of occasions." How rare the person who really knows, and affirms with certainty! And how infectious stammering and hesitating and doubting are!

5. *Analysis.* The analytical power is sharpened, the synthetic enfeebled. The analysts wait until you speak to analyze you to smithereens; they hardly speak first themselves, they hardly put forward a positive position—they hardly propose a proposition. Element after element is brought out and set forth side by side. The mystery of the whole which these elements originally constitute is not wondered at. There is an element of magic here; in fact one task would be to identify in detail the spirit of superstition and magic which pervades modern thought. It would be a fascinating investigation. The dominance of analysis is a phenomenon of materialism; because materialism in the final analysis is finding rest in the lower and simpler, and hoping that somehow the mere passage of time and agglomeration of the elements will, as by magic, give rise, or has given rise, to the higher and more complex.

In philosophy there is first the singling out of the one element of language and then the endless analyzing of this element. The mystery of the whole of human existence from which this one element has been detached and analyzed *ad nauseam* is then proclaimed as nonsense. Pascal points out that the mathematician is apt to think of you—you the living-dying human being —as a proposition!

Another task—also a fascinating one—would be to wonder at the mystery of how linguistic analysis under the inspiration of Ludwig Wittgenstein has dominated Anglo-Saxon thought. Who is not a Wittgensteinian today, just as who is not a Freudian or a Marxist? In much of the humanities, and not only in philosophy, linguistic analysis and the spirit of Wittgenstein today reign supreme. The linguistic quest of meaning has ended up in the whole from which language has been chopped out, losing all meaning.

6. *Idealism.* This is a form of rationalism, but it is active in the sense that people dedicate themselves to an idea and mobilize all their powers to realize it. All reformers, all revolutionaries, all votaries of a "cause," are idealists. The active idealists invariably cluster together under some leader; they actively seek and enlist converts; they form parties, societies, "movements." The ideal is conceived as wholly manmade. Movements fired by an ideal fight each other ferociously. They recognize and know no peace among themselves. The student of the humanities receives, sometimes tendentiously, sometimes uncritically, generous fares of diverse kinds of idealism, militant or academic, in his sojourn at the university.

7. *Materialism.* Theoretically, this means the reduction of everything, in the final analysis, to matter in motion and to the space in which it moves; this is Democritus and Lucretius. In terms of concrete existence, this means economism, that is, the derivation of everything about man from the ruthless economic struggle. Here materialism joins hands with Marxism and with the atheistic stripe of socialism. Freudianism, Marxism and socialism compete with one another for the domination of the mind of the humanities, and often they interpenetrate and support one another. There is no phenomenon more remarkable today than

how the thought of the humanities is seized by materialism, Freudianism, Marxism and socialism. The total and absolute and original independence of thought and spirit from the materialist factor however conceived is not affirmed by the humanities. And when an organic interaction between the two is recognized, matter is always conceived as original and spirit as derivative— Marx's notion of epiphenomenon. There is a subtle fear that unless you do so you will land in some God, and hence in the Bible and in Jesus Christ; and this must be avoided at all costs.

8. *Technologism.* The humanities are to be technicized, instrumentalized; they are to be reduced to the realm of means. "What is the use" of history, literature, religion, art, philosophy, etc.? The "use" is sought outside these accomplishments altogether. It is not enough that you, as a living human being, be a historically cultured person, one who is soaked in the giants of thought and literature, a religious man or woman who knows and worships the Holy Trinity, who is sensitive to and loves great beauty and art, who converses deeply on the great issues of life. Your perfection in these things, in and for themselves, is not the end. The end is the "use" of them, that they be used as means. And so you assimilate the humanities to the realm of technology; you resort to graphs, charts, models, striking analyses, mathematical formulas, to impress and catch the attention of your audience, to make the humanities relevant and useful, to advertise your wares, to sell your products. The technological virus has infected the realm of thought and spirit. And thereby the peace, the beauty, the grace, the power, the rest, the sufficiency, the being of thought and spirit have disappeared.

9. *Futurism.* So far as any positive moral guidance is afforded by the humanities, it is the control of the future. Prepare for the future, think of the future, concentrate on the future, orient

yourself to the future, plan for the future, get ready for your career, scan the job market. Nothing objectionable in all this if it were not pure formalism without content. The doctrine of development has taken such hold on the mind since the San Francisco Conference of 1945 that the whole world is now divided into developed and developing nations.[3] For both, but especially for the developing, the future is the lure. The future then is the thing, and nothing judging past, present and future from outside them altogether. Man finds his existential condition intolerable, and so he flees into the future in the hope that he will thus escape from himself. But there is no possible escape from himself, and, poor man! his condition is going to keep bedeviling him every step of the way.

III

10. *Cynicism.* There is also a great deal of cleverness, calculation and cynicism in the humanities. Genuineness is in very short supply. Cynicism and nihilism always go together, but cynicism is more original. In the humanities today one seeks in vain for the great and confident mind that takes a firm and sustained stand on the great issues of life and death and purpose and meaning and being, both theoretically and in responsible personal living; I mean a mind who would be respected by an Aristotle or a Goethe, a mind whom these men would love to meet and converse with. In business and in the technological world one finds such minds, and in their own spheres they are respected, but very rarely in the realm of the humanities. What meets us here is for the most part the chilling smile of the cynic who takes pleasure in nothing, who dismisses everything, even the most momentous, as of no importance, who enjoys the game of elaborating endless arguments which invariably end up in the total obfuscation of what is discussed. Darkness, uncertainty, in-

security, the dissolution of being into not-being, the "vanity of vanities, all is vanity" of Ecclesiastes—this is the mood and fundamental attitude; and this is invariably the outcome. The lips are not firm, there is not even laughter: there is only that soul-scorching awful smile.

11. *Nihilism.* It is incredible how much the spirit of nihilism pervades the humanities today. We said since everything changes and only the moment counts, the end result of the most brilliant discourse is nothing—a passing momentary pleasure; or a revulsion if it happens to rub us the wrong way. Pull down and annihilate everything that is: customs, traditions, institutions, establishments, revered values, the sensibilities of parents, the names of the great, the classical norms. The rule, the intent, is to debunk everything. And while you are not in power yourself, pull down those who are. The spirit of destroying everything stalks the earth. The malicious pleasure in destruction is one of the most deep-seated impulses in human nature: it is Satanic. How much we take pleasure in even the unmerited misfortunes of others! It is ontological murder, and man has been a murderer since Cain.

12. *Freudianism.* If rationalism worships reason and voluntarism the will, Freudianism worships the third side of man: his biological equipment, his dreams and drives. Sex here plays a dominant role. How much Freud contributed to the phenomenon of what is called "the sexual revolution of the age" is a theme to be considered—again a fascinating one. Unless mercilessly exposed and exploded, this Freudian sexual onslaught, contributing to the total breakdown of morals and disintegration of the family, could destroy Western civilization. And yet the universities seem to revel in it.

Literature is predominantly Freudian; much literary criticism is Freudian when it is not Marxist. No one is free today from the taint of Freud. The important thing common to all these revolutions is that they all pour into the one stream of the Great Counterrevolution: everything must be done to divert attention from Jesus Christ, whether by causing us to dwell on and sink in our dreams and drives, or by turning our attention to what are called social conditions, or by obfuscating the language we use, or by whipping up in us the will to power, or by putting before us the lure of the future; anything and everything except Jesus Christ and the cross.

13. *Relativism.* This is the polyheaded hydra of Plato: it assumes a thousand forms; you extirpate one head here, soon it sprouts again elsewhere. Relativism has nothing to do with the theory of relativity of Einstein; Einstein's accomplishment is a solid scientific one. But morally there is in the humanities today an almost complete relativization of all truth, all value and all worth. The good is what you can get away with, what subserves—provided you can get away with it—your momentary impulse or purpose or interest. Only the moment counts. You are in the presence of no transcendent Judge whatever. That there is a Day of Judgment in some life beyond, or even in this life (upon your children, for example) is nonsense. "Society" will take care of the children! Fear nothing: fear no retribution, no God. Fear only scandal, and provided you take the necessary precautions against scandal (i.e., against "society," and with the aid of countless ingenious technological devices, this is relatively easy today), the sky is the limit for what you can do. Morality is situational, circumstantial, relative, and nothing more. Everything can be justified as having been occasioned by the situation.

14. *Voluntarism.* Everything, including reason, is brushed aside before the will. The will determines everything: this is the teaching of Schopenhauer and Nietzsche. It is rooted in Leib-

niz and German Idealism. It is a fundamental presupposition of Marx. Pascal refers to it as a frailty to be guarded against. Sartre proclaims, "I create myself." And our youth speak of nothing more than of what *they want*.

15. *Change*. Everything changes. Only change does not change, or it changes only in the rate of change—in accelerating or decelerating. The mind rests on nothing final, firm, given, solid, unchanging. The mere thought of an existing, judging absolute is sheer fantasy. In the humanities today the ultimate principle which seems to satisfy the soul of the humanist is the persuasion, Everything changes. Why this or that development or new phenomenon, you ask. Well, comes the answer, everything changes. This is a form of fatalism. No sadness, no regret, no sense of tragedy. Change is God.

16. *In a Hurry*. The humanities, both students and professors, are in a hurry. They must get somewhere! God knows where! They cannot rest where they are! "Be still, and know that I am God,"[4] that they hardly know. Stillness, which belongs to the essence of the humanities, has been distilled out of them altogether. The deadline must be met, the manuscript must be completed, the dissertation must be revised, the meeting must be attended, the appointment must be kept, the news must be followed, the developments must be watched, the latest literature must be mastered, their anxieties about their position and their future must be allayed—and therefore they can give you only five minutes! And even in these five minutes their mind is not on you. There is no stillness, no quiet, no rest, no living in the presence of eternity, no overcoming of time and its pressures, no unfretting patience, no resting in being just yourself. "The peace which passeth all understanding" is beyond reach, nay beyond understanding. They must be on the go all the time. Again, on the go where?—God knows.

But the humanities mean peace, grace, patience, communion with others, the joys of fellowship and sharing, the art of relaxed, creative conversation, abiding friendship, love—love of the subject matter and love of your friends—the suspension of time, forgetting even yourself, that incredible inner freedom which creates on the spot, God knows how and God knows from where.

17. *Humanism*. Man is the most important visible creature, but humanism does not mean just this assertion. There certainly is such a thing as "Christian humanism" which is totally different from the humanism of the humanists; for how can there be no "Christian humanism" when God himself, according to Christian belief, became man? How can there be no "Christian humanism" when man became divine in Jesus Christ? Christian humanism is grounded in the Son of God who is at the same time the Son of man. Without the Son of man there is no man to speak of—except an ambiguous being tending to, thirsting for, the Son of man.

The humanism of which we speak here is the worship of man and his powers alone. Humanism is the affirmation of the absolute self-sufficiency of man. What Pascal perpetually refers to as the wretchedness, the misery, of man, humanism affects to know nothing about. But since this wretchedness is a fact, how can we still *worship* man? Man can solve every problem, man needs no aid from outside—in fact there is no "outside" to seek aid from. Can he solve his suffering, can he solve his anxiety, can he solve his loneliness, can he solve his meanness, can he solve his maliciousness, can he solve his rebelliousness, can he solve his "bad luck," can he solve his resentment, can he solve his fear, can he solve his death? Humanism is atheism; it is the denial of the sovereign and independent God. It is the deification, not of "the universe," but of man. Humanism does not know how wretched man is; the humanist does not know how wretched he is; or he knows and simply cannot bear it. Being a rebel, he turns his gaze away from his wretchedness. Humanism is inveterate human pride and rebellion. The humanities have turned humanist; and since there is no real man without God, the humanities have turned antihuman.

18. *Monism.* This is the problem of the numbers two and one. The whole temper of the humanities is that one is the basic number and not two. There is one all-embracing whole, be it "the universe," or "nature," or "matter," or "man," or "reason," or "the will to power," or something even if it should turn out to be nothing (Heidegger in one of his moods). Monism is simply reductionism; there is no room for an unbridgeable gap; everything should be reduced to some oneness; everything is controllable. The original healthy wonder at being as being is gradually being blunted by subjectivism, idealism and monism. The really "other," let alone "the wholly other," does not exist. God is man's creation rather than man God's (Feuerbach). Monism in all its forms is the acme of human pride. Mortal man knowing his incurable finitude should be ashamed of himself. He knows it but he does not admit it. Man is a rebel against himself and therefore against God; more originally, against God and therefore against himself.

19. *Immanentism.* Immanentism is the denial of genuine transcendence. The transcendence of Heidegger and Jaspers is all fake. The whole notion of "the above," "the beyond," "the other," is absent. The causes of all things are already there on the same drab plane. The radically above is nonsense: it can be brought down to the same level of the given. The radically beyond is nonsense: it will sooner or later be overtaken. The radically other is a notion of sheer lunacy. We are taught by God

that "the fear of God is the beginning of wisdom," but immanentism knows no ontological "fear" whatever. It also knows
no awe, no wonder, no sense of mystery, no dread, no possibility of surprise. The notion of the worldly, the profane, the
temporal, the secular, the lay, as opposed to the sacred, the holy,
the religious, the spiritual, the eternal, the "wholly other," has
almost completely vanished. "And he said, Draw not nigh
hither: put off thy shoes from off thy feet, for the place whereon
thou standest is holy ground."⁵ Is there any "holy ground" left
in the humanities today? You can put on your shoes and tread
anywhere you please. There is nothing to desecrate since there
is nothing holy.

20. *Secularism*. *Saecularis* means the generation, the age,
the times, the world. Therefore secularism is to be beholden
to, to be bound to, the times in which we live. In this sense
secularism is almost identical with modernism. It has kinship
also to the *Zeitgeist*. While there is a sharp distinction today
between the secular and the religious, in an age of faith the distinction would not be absolute because the worldly would be
subordinate to the religious. When we say therefore that the
humanities reflect a secularist spirit, we simply mean that they
are infused with the spirit of the age which is wholly unspiritual.
The Spirit as an original, independent, inscrutable potency is
alien to the times in which we live, and the humanities have
succumbed to the times.

21. *Atheism*. The cumulative effect of all these fundamental
attitudes is atheism—the outright denial of God as conceived
and believed in by Judaism, Christianity and Islam. When
Pascal exclaims, "The God of Abraham, of Isaac and of Jacob,
and not the God of the philosophers," the humanities stand
aghast. The more militant will deny God's existence altogether;
the more tolerant will take to deism; both would declare him

wholly irrelevant to the enterprise of the humanities. The atheism of the age reflects itself in the atheism of the humanities, and the atheism of the humanities in turn rationalizes and confirms the atheism of the age. There is no distinctive Christian content in the subject matter of the curricula: it is unquestioningly taken for granted that such content has no place in them. When the Bible is included, it is taught as "literature," and there is a studied design to choose the portions which are devoid of any doctrinal content. The poetry of it is brought out and nothing of the material content and faith of the living-dying authors. What, then, is the material content of the curricula? Invariably something rationalist, humanist, relativist, Freudian, immanentist, secularist.

IV

I have always wanted to write an essay on the sway of superstition and magic in these enlightened and progressive times. It will set forth the evidence of how much educated people, even scientists and thinkers, believe in luck, accident, chance, fate, fortune. We tell people when we bid them forth on a mission "good luck," and we speak of their having met with a "bad fortune" when their mission proved a failure. The point is not the use of these terms, which, though heathen in origin, are still innocuous, but that we use them and stop there. Who does not speculate and gamble and take risks, and not only with respect to the stock market where he has placed his investments? Of a piece with this is the vogue of Indian thought and practice (and not only among the middle-aged and elderly), including expecting salvation from drugs and from the manipulation of the body. Freud and his school speak of "sexual liberation"; this too is a species of magic, because in reality this "liberation" is certain enslavement, and when it is far advanced and the habits formed cannot be humanly broken, it conduces to death, both moral, spiritual and physical. Of a piece also is the craze about the horoscope.

There is an element of magic also in the prevalence of probability, statistics, the law of averages, in scientific doctrine and practice today. Of course there are situations where, scientifically, one can only talk in terms of probability. But it is not much (at least not sufficient) comfort for an anxious patient to tell him, for example, that the treatment he is receiving has been statistically shown to be curative in seventy (or even ninety) percent of similar cases, and therefore his "chance" of total recovery is seventy (or even ninety) percent. What if his "luck" (a "bad" one indeed) should fall under the remaining thirty (or even ten) percent? Even if the probability were ninety-nine percent, the remaining one percent would still hang over his head as a sword of Damocles.

The vogue of what is called "emergent evolution" (Lloyd Morgan and others) or "creative evolution" (Bergson, Whitehead and others) illustrates the same point. To speak of novelty "emerging" is perfectly legitimate, but the question remains: "emerging" how, "emerging" from where? Examine closely Morgan and his school and you will find they do not really know the "how," and as to the "from where" the answer is "from nowhere." Magic, darkness, sorcery, nothingness, here reign. And the notion of "creation" in Bergson and Whitehead is but a subterfuge for their underlying monistic dogma that the universe, as a total process and as individual events, is self-creative.

The difference between "the nothing" of the believer who says God creates "from nothing," and "the nothing" of these thinkers who say the universe creates itself "from nothing," is that to the believer God, the fullness of being, already exists, and he created the world not from himself nor from some pre-existent material, but by his mere willing word, "Be!", and that the creature is "wholly other" than the Creator; whereas "the nothing" of these philosophers is a way of saying that God as the church and the Bible know and affirm him does not exist and that universe, creator, creature, thinker, are all one thing "in process of self-creation."

Similarly, there is magic and superstition, there is fundamental orientation towards darkness and not-being, there is a species of witchcraft, when the Marxists say that beyond a certain amount quantity mutates into quality. You ask, how can this be? They answer: So it is! In other words, they just will it so. The will to power!

So there are two acts of willing: one by God who absolutely exists but is wholly other than the world and the thinker and any outcome of his willing; and the other by the human thinker who only relatively exists, because he is mortal and fallible, but also wills, and since he cannot create anything from nothing, he simply wills (really, wishes) that he and the universe be one in self-sufficiency and self-creation. God exists; he does not create himself; he creates things wholly other than himself. Proud man thinks he creates himself and projects this thought onto "the universe" in such a way as to conceive the universe either as self-creative like himself or as itself created by himself —all to escape the thought that he and everything in "the universe" are creatures from nothing by the word of God, all to avoid "giving God the praise"!

People also resort to all sorts of clever tricks (they call them psychological), both in the language they use and in their dealings with others; and whatever results they then get they attribute to the efficacy of the tricks. I marvel at times at the lack of reserve, at the prodigality, with which "the Lord" is invoked by some people—doubtless well-meaning people but misguided and dazed. This is magic and they call it "the Lord." Some advertising displays considerable magic.

All these instances are a tiny fraction of the total evidence of the hold of magic and superstition on the contemporary mind.

We are then in the presence of a despairing soul waiting, not on the Lord, as David would have us do, but on nothing, a mind literally expecting something from nothing, a mind jumping into the dark with closed eyes to scoop something from nowhere. Trust in luck, trust in fate, burn incense at the altar of the goddess Fortuna, and you will be "surprised" how well it will go with you. And when you are not "surprised" you are admonished to try again and again. The principle of all this is expecting something from nothing, and this is exactly the meaning of magic. The phenomenon is the worship of sheer nothingness, utter darkness, pure not-being. The role of nothing in modern thought is absolutely amazing, and this role must be analyzed and exposed. Heidegger in a famous address in 1933 expounded the power of nothing in human thought, and Karl Barth in his *Church Dogmatics* commented critically on this exposition. At some point the connection of being is broken. And then—a cry of despair! Existentially this is an expression of unutterable loneliness, a dreadful cry for fellowship and love. With invisible demons floating about us everywhere all the time, Augustine would call it a mode of demonic possession.[6]

I am not saying that our age is more demonically seized, more parched for love and fellowship, than former times. I am saying that it is not less magic-beholden, not less superstitious, not less oriented toward nothingness and not-being (the *to mai on* of Plato), than ages past. This is the eternal human condition: man can never get over, he can never progress beyond, his direst need for help from outside himself and outside "the universe" altogether.

In a work recently published entitled *The Controversial Kierkegaard* there is a passage which I wish to quote here apropos of what I am discussing, without any commentary:

Here we see Kierkegaard's pseudonym already attacking the watered-down Protestant piety that has degenerated into secularism. This is no less a live issue in our day, when the results of secularism and paganism within Protestantism and other church denominations continually become more apparent. What it actually means is that instead of a valuing of inward deepening there is a tendency toward the demonic. In one of his later journals, Kierkegaard drastically depicts one of the advanced results of this movement toward the demonic:

"In contrast to what was said about possession in the Middle Ages and times like that, that there were individuals who sold themselves to the devil, I have an urge to write a book: Possession and Obsession in Modern Times, and show how people *en masse* abandon themselves to it, how it is now carried on *en masse*. That is why people run together in flocks—so that natural and animal rage will grip a person, so that he feels stimulated, inflamed, and *ausser sich* [outside himself]. The scenes on Bloksberg are utterly pedantic compared to this demonic lust, a lust to lose oneself in order to evaporate in a potentiation, so that a person is outside of himself, does not really know what he is doing or what he is saying or who it is or what it is speaking through him, while the blood rushes faster, the eyes glitter and stare fixedly, the passions boil, lusts seethe.

"What depth of confusion and corruption, when at the same time it is praised as the earnestness of life, as cordiality, love, yes—as Christianity."[7]

It is very significant that the first concrete example of a demonic state cited by Johannes de Silentio, namely, the merman, is drawn from the domain of the erotic. Kierkegaard saw very clearly how the erotic, the sexual, can lead a person into the demonic. In our day as well, we have seen how certain psychological theories, primarily Freud's psychoanalysis, have extensively promoted sexual liberation as a means to greater personal development. In actuality this so-called liberation is a movement towards the demonic in that it must be regarded as a more or less hidden revolt against Christianity's requirement of the dominion of spirit over the sensate.[8]

V

Am I saying, then, that all the humanities—history, literature, philosophy, psychology, etc.—are equally humanist-relativist-Freudian-immanentist? I am not.

Am I saying that there are no genuinely believing professors in the humanities who joyously practice their faith? I am not.

Am I saying that there are no genuinely believing students in the humanities who joyously practice their faith and whose faith survives the humanist onslaught when they graduate? I am not.

Am I saying that the great universities in Europe and the Western hemisphere are not producing first-class works in the sciences and the humanities and are not training fine young men and women who in time become great scientists, scholars, humanists, philosophers, thinkers? I am not.

Am I saying that there are no professors in predominantly humanist-secularist universities who give excellent courses in the humanities in which the door is left open for Jesus Christ and authentic spiritual values? I am not.

Am I saying that the universities are not inviting great Christian scholars to lecture on strictly Christian themes? I am not.

Am I saying that the general education curriculum in the great secular universities is of no value from the Christian point of view? I am not.

Am I saying that the present widespread debate in the American academic community with respect to the place, value, character and content of liberal education, a debate that manifests itself in diverse forms, sometimes conscious, sometimes subtle, sometimes in violent attack, sometimes in mere silence or in silent wonder, sometimes in concerned search, is of no value from the Christian point of view? I am not.

Am I saying that the secularist-humanist university tradition of the last several centuries has not made great progress in precision, criticism, width and depth of comprehension, and in the refinement of the canons and standards of research and scholarship, and the elevation of the quality of the products of such research and scholarship? I am not.

I am saying (a) that there is no distinctively Christian content in the curricula; (b) that this secularism appears to be a studied policy; (c) that the diverse determinations enumerated above characterize every department of the humanities in varying combinations and modes of subordination; (d) that the believing professor or student will continue practicing his belief, when he does, not thanks to any religious reinforcement he receives from the disciplines of the humanities in which he is engaged; (e) that whatever spiritual nurture the believing student or professor receives comes to him from outside the university; (f) that the dominant atmosphere, climate, spirit, outlook, attitude in the universities of Europe, Canada and America is rationalist-relativist-humanist-monist-immanentist; (g) that this dominant atmosphere and climate is distinctly and consciously hostile to anything that has any reference, direct or indirect, to God, Jesus Christ and the Spirit; (h) that sometimes it forbids the very mention of the Name; (i) that in the university the struggle for survival of faith among the believing professors and students is incredibly harsh and discouraging; (j) that very few survive this struggle unscathed; and (k) that these few, when they exist, are among the veritable spiritual heroes of our times. Such has been the total divorce between God, Jesus Christ, the Spirit, the Bible, the saints, the great cumulative tradition, worship, mystery, "the fear of the Lord," on the one hand, and the humanities which mold the mind and character of tens of millions of youths every year, on the other!

VI

If you are taught day and night, either explicitly or by presupposition, that in the end of ends there is nothing except matter in motion; that we are essentially dust and to dust we shall return; that truth, even with a small "t," does not exist; that nothing is certain, nothing secure; that the last word is what Whitehead calls process, the welter, flux, passage; that philosophy is only a matter of linguistic analysis; that all metaphysics is nonsense; that the great issues of life and death, of being and becoming, of suffering and destiny, of knowledge and truth, which preoccupied Plato, Aristotle, Augustine, Saint Thomas, Kant and Nietzsche, are so many linguistic obfuscations which can be readily demonstrated as nonsense by linguistic analysis; that essentially life has no meaning; that if life has any meaning it is to eat and drink and be merry, and to extend your power and control; that all values are relative to custom and culture; that there is no absolute beauty, no absolute justice, no absolute love, no absolute mercy; that morality is private or at best situational; that right is ultimately only what you can safely get away with; that man is essentially his dreams and drives; that the judgment that might is right is the deepest and most determinant insight in politics; that politics and economics alone determine the course of history; that freedom in art is to disfigure the human figure (Picasso); that God is man or matter or reason or the will or technology or nothing; and that the God of religion, if he exists, is irrelevant; and not only that; but if you have also to pass examinations on all these themes, and, if you are writing a doctoral dissertation, to pore over the voluminous literature of such teaching for years; then, is it any wonder that, after eight or ten years (the most formative in your life) of such rigorous drilling in the university, you become thoroughly brainwashed into the rationalist-relativist-naturalist-Freudian-sophistical-monistic-immanentist-atheistic cast of mind? And parents wring their hands and complain about what is happening to their children; and thinkers keep on only "thinking"; and leaders wonder at the decadence all around them and perhaps also in them; and churches appear unconcerned, except to continue preaching the gospel, as though there was not also such a momentous thing as the independent *problem of the university* with which they, too, and in the name of the gospel itself, should be concerned!

A Christian critique of the university must point out the absence of Jesus Christ from the curricula of the humanities. This absence is today so much taken as a matter of course that even to hint at it is to provoke the wrath of the humanities and to invite a thousand learned rebuttals. A Christian critique is presumably carried out by a Christian, and a Christian stands in the presence of Jesus Christ. How can a Christian critic fail to notice the conspicuous absence of that in whose presence he constantly lives and moves and has his being? The university, a world of thought all by itself entirely apart from Christ? Christ to be relegated merely to the family, to the church, to private feeling? He is wholly to be forbidden entry into the halls of learning of the greatest universities? This is the issue.

CHAPTER SIX

SOME PROBLEMS

THERE ARE A FEW BASIC problems which call for deeper consideration.

I

Knowledge is power, as Bacon remarked, and with the increase of knowledge, both quantitatively and qualitatively, there is increase of power. Think of the power which the holders of the secret of the nucleus and the gene can wield today! There is then the problem of some original value, some original deterring power, some original compassion, some original fear of God or of something, which will guide and restrain the holders of such immense power. If all is relative, if all is dust, if there is no hidden judge, if there is only the will to power, if resentment can vent itself without restraint, if the pleasure of the exercise of power can be enjoyed with no regard for value, no fear of retribution (and how often some statesmen in our time, commanding great power but acting as pure operators and balancers, have permitted whole cultures, whole venerable traditions, whole free societies, to be destroyed or subjugated, just to remain in control themselves!), or with only the retribution of calculated self-destruction, then let me destroy the world (Is there any greater pleasure than this ultimate exercise of power?), if I can, even if I should destroy myself with it (á la Samson), or let me sport with the most fantastic projects of "genetic engineering" (Is there anything more thrilling than that?). Who is going to supply the necessary restraint, the necessary fear, the necessary compassion, against this unbounded willfulness of man? All these holders of immense power are products of the university, and if the dominant spirit of the university continues to be hostile to, or even indifferent to, absolute spiritual values, then God help the future of mankind.

There is, second, the problem of wholeness, of order, not only among the sciences, but principally in concrete, existential, personal living, with the myriad stimuli and demands that impinge upon the finite soul every day. (Who has time to finish reading even what he must strictly read for his own interests in *The New York Times* or *Time* magazine?) There is no respite or rest in sight; in fact there is perpetual acceleration. In this maddening world, who can give us the necessary rest, the poised perspective, the necessary wholeness of soul, the necessary unity of mind? I doubt that these can be secured in the great universities today. If the agencies which principally control the mind of the world and therefore the world itself today are helpless to introduce any real, lasting wholeness into human existence which issues in joy and hope and certainty and power, and if they do not appear to be making the necessary effort to overcome this defect, then again God help the future of mankind!

Third, the marvels of modern transportation and communication have brought together more diverse people than ever before. One place where they congregate is the university, another is international conferences, a third is the great urban centers. The problem of linguistic communication has been resolved, partly by technological devices, partly by the English language becoming the lingua franca of the world, more than any other language in history since the Tower of Babel. No language in history ever carried a greater moral responsibility for the kind of message and meaning and direction of mind it articulated to the whole world than the English language today.

But there is a deeper problem, namely, the problem of sharing fundamental attitudes, faith and convictions, especially with people whose fundamental attitudes, faith and convictions not only differ from our own but consciously contradict them and aim at effacing them altogether from history. More than ever before in history we are thrown together with such people (certainly in the halls of learning) in the same room or gathering or conference every day. The problem here is the inhibition which we naturally feel of not daring to share with the other person the deepest we know and believe. The conversation remains more or less on the level of the weather and the latest gossip. This is what I call the problem of the least common denominator: are we by nature fated to suppress and never express the deepest we know lest we offend?

The classes and gatherings in the great universities are invariably mixed audiences (universities are international and intercultural), and in many such meetings we are not supposed to express religious, and sometimes political, opinions and convictions that could have a divisive effect. In this way the deepest religious convictions are automatically ruled out from these halls. Only secularist-rationalist-humanist-immanentist topics are allowed. But we soon get fed up with that, if we are people of faith, and we soon itch for deeper communion, which we can never expect in the class or lecture room, or even privately between us and our classmates or professors or colleagues.

A basic principle of the university is responsible freedom of expression (and expression is not only intellectual-verbal but in the first instance behavioral-existential) even, indeed especially, about the deepest one knows, but this does not apply to religious or sometimes even political conviction in formal university gatherings. If the deepest one knows is perpetually suppressed, it rusts and atrophies. There is no thought of casting our pearls indiscriminately and on any occasion, but there is a most painful problem here: we are never fully ourselves! And who can exist while the fullness of his or her being is perpetually cramped?

Who, then, can help the religious soul in the great universities, the soul that craves the freedom of full being, who can help it to bear the pain of unfreedom, to control its feelings, to refrain from expressing itself at the wrong moment (compare the daemon of Socrates); and who can grant it the grace and humility of saying the right word *(le mot propre)* at the right time? Only a Dostoyevski can depict these situations adequately and with the requisite compassion. I am thinking of *The Idiot.*

II

There is, fourth, the tremendous problem of whether there is essential incompatibility between reason and faith, between knowledge and virtue, between scholarship and the sense of mystery. On the face of it there seems to be such incompatibility. Can we give ourselves totally to Jesus Christ and the life of contemplation and still create intellectually? Aren't you jarred out of yourself every time you move (or are forcibly interrupted) from the wonderful peace of contemplation even to active love (helping and serving those in need), let alone to the scholarly pursuit? Don't you feel then that you have landed in a different world altogether, indeed in an antithetical world? Can you serve two masters at the same time—thought and the resurrected Christ?

It appears that something must be sacrificed here. We admire the accomplishments of the great scholars and philosophers, but we are not impressed by their spiritual state. They appear to lack grace, humility, contrition, love, joy, perhaps even feeling. We are not sure they have a heart; we are not sure they are human; we find ourselves before a being possessed and consumed by his "idea," a being who has offered his soul at the altar of his "idea" (à la Faust). I cannot imagine an Aristotle or a Kant or a Hegel falling on his knees, confessing his sins (does he have any?) and smiting his breast. I do not feel they can understand a great psalm when they read it, let alone the eighth chapter of St. Paul's Epistle to the Romans or the fourth chapter of St. John's First Epistle. And yet the intellectual accomplishments of some of these scholars and philosophers are outstanding, and some of them receive the Nobel Prize in their own fields.

Conversely, how meek and simple and spiritual and transparent some of the saints or saintly are, and yet how unsophisticated and wholly uninteresting and illiterate when it comes to sharing the great philosophical or scientific or world problems! We sit at their feet spiritually, but intellectually they are babes; they simply bore you; we cannot stay long with them; we crave the company of great intellects. None of them qualifies for a Nobel Prize for his intellectual achievement; Mother Teresa of Calcutta received it not for her intellect but for her incredible love.

So there is a problem here; truth and knowledge cannot be alien to Jesus Christ, the Eternal Logos; and yet the more we know scientific and philosophical truth the more we seem to be alienated from him; and the more we cling to him in love the more our intellectual grasp of scientific and philosophical truth appears to suffer, and the less we can converse with the great minds on an equal footing. Mind and spirit appear to be two radically different worlds; they do not understand each other; they cannot communicate, let alone commune, with one another; they are not at ease in the presence of one another; they profoundly disturb one another; each wishes the other did not exist; each hates the sight of the other; each wishes to be left alone. The spirit looks upon the pursuits of the mind as pointless and futile; the wisdom of the world is foolishness with God; and the mind looks down upon the spirit as primitive, ignorant, stupid, pitiful.

I can only say we must trust the mercy and love of Christ even in this impossible situation. But the problem is there and even this trust does not cause it to evaporate.

Fifth, the university is only a microcosm of the world. The prevailing values of the macrocosm get focused in the microcosm. A Christian critique of the university is indirectly a Christian critique of contemporary Western civilization. When the full Christian critique of the university is elaborated, it will inevitably turn out to be a full Christian critique of the world as well. Christ is judging both, the macrocosm and the microcosm. Neither is independent of the other. Christ is passing judgment on the secularism, immanentism, monism, rationalism, relativism, Freudianism, etc., of both the world and the university. And yet the world is too amorphous to afford us a handle with which to get hold of it, other than by the church continuing to proclaim, in season and out of season, the gospel of sin, repentance and salvation through Jesus Christ.

The university is a clear-cut fulcrum with which to move the world. The problem here is for the church to realize that no greater service can it render both itself and the cause of the gospel, with which it is entrusted, than to try to recapture the universities for Christ on whom they were all originally founded. One of the best ways of treating the macrocosm is through the handle of the universities in which millions of youths destined to positions of leadership spend, in rigorous training, between four and ten years of the most formative period of their life. More potently than by any other means, change the university and you change the world.

This means much more, however, than converting a student here and changing a professor there; such converting and changing, while necessary and while it must continue, is peripheral and rather pathetic when it comes to the real character and magnitude of the task; those who interpret the challenge of the university only in these terms miss the whole point; they are either not university graduates themselves, or, if they are, they failed to grasp the meaning of the phrase "the state of the mind and the spirit in the university as a whole"; the "wholeness" of university existence has escaped them.

It means, rather, responsible concern for the contents of the curriculum, how the curriculum came to be what it is, the kind of ideas, attitudes, fundamental interpretation of history and society and man and morals and destiny and being it imparts; it means thinking of the central university policy, regardless of whether it came about by drift or by design, thinking of the kind of spiritual climate and frame of mind it fosters as an *ongoing rooted institution* both by the topics and practices it includes and the topics and practices it excludes.

All this is a world of concern by itself quite independent of holding evangelizing crusades on the campus, or helping meet individual moral problems of students or professors, or setting up prayer or Bible study groups among members of the university community, or promoting Christian fellowship for the lonely and neglected, or bringing a student here and a student there on his knees before Jesus Christ. All these endeavors are praiseworthy and necessary, but the problem of the university is other than and much more formidable than all of them. It is whether the intellect can be totally independent of Jesus Christ and remain sound and sane and true. It is whether a necessary condition for the highest creativity of the intellect is precisely to have nothing to do with Jesus Christ.

III

Then in the sixth place, there is the question of presumption. We said the ultimate judge is Jesus Christ himself and we are seeking his judgment of the university. We said in this inquiry we attach no importance to our opinion but only to the judgment of Jesus Christ. Is it not presumptuous on our part, it would be objected, to claim that we know the opinion of Jesus Christ? Who are we to make this claim, we who have repeatedly reproached mankind, ourselves, for our fallibility, mortality and subjection to a thousand and one whims and corruptions, and asked ourselves bluntly to be ashamed and repent of our pride of knowledge? "Physician, heal thyself," it would be said, and snap out of your presumption and pride! Here are ten brief observations on this matter of presumption.

(a) The question, What does Jesus Christ think of the university? is perfectly clear and valid. It may not have an answer, but it can be legitimately asked. At least so far forth, then, we are incurring no presumption in raising it.

(b) The mere mention of Jesus Christ disturbs, not because the question cannot be answered, or even raised, but because the academic community has for generations now succeeded in convincing itself that it has at last once and for all outgrown that very question. (As we pointed out above, this is what is ultimately meant by "progress" and "liberation.") Therefore the odium of presumption does not fall on us, who without presumption simply ask the question, but on the academic community that presumptuously dogmatizes that the matter has long since been settled forever.

(c) Even those who do not believe, as we do, that Jesus Christ is living in himself, but who nevertheless allow some validity to what they call Christian principles and morals, could ask the question and seek an answer to it on the basis of these very principles and morals. They could write a whole intelligible critique of the university on that basis.

(d) We said all along that we have ventured to undertake this whole inquiry in fear and trembling. Because of its supreme importance it should be undertaken despite every possibility of error. The university more than any institution dominates the world, and we can allow no fear, no trembling, no difficulty to weaken our resolve. One attitude could be that, because the greater the issue the greater the risk of error, therefore let us desist from exploring where angels fear to tread. Our conclusion is the exact opposite: because of its critical bearing on every other issue, the great issue of the university demands that we examine it regardless of any possible pitfalls on the way. All the same, we pursue it in total fear and trembling, which means, confidently and in the living presence of Jesus Christ.

(e) We certainly may err in reading Christ's mind on this matter, but if there is Jesus Christ and if there is his Holy Spirit and if we are open to him, he will, at his pleasure, correct our error and guide us into the truth. This is much more than a mere subjectivist, formal statement: we are wholly open to the correction of others who seek him and live in his presence.

(f) This correction is decisive since we are open to the entire cumulative tradition. I think I know enough of the Old and the

New Testaments, especially of the Psalms and the four Gospels and the writings of Paul, Peter and John, of the great saints, such as Augustine, Chrysostom, Basil, Ephrem, John of Damascus, Aquinas and Teresa, and of the great Protestant theologians, such as Jonathan Edwards and Karl Barth, and I am sufficiently steeped in the Greek Orthodox liturgy and tradition, to feel quite confident that my reading of the will of Christ on the subject of the university is not egregiously off the mark. All these people believed in the living will of Christ and sought it and trusted that he would reveal it to them. If any important element in this vast tradition should contradict any of my fundamental propositions here, I would construe that to be a signal for me to reconsider my position. Those who speak of presumption could have a point if they were Christian and if they knew as much as I do of this immense tradition; in that case I would sit at their feet and learn from them; in that case neither they nor I would speak of presumption, but only of love and fellowship and sharing and common concern; and we would certainly agree on what Jesus Christ thinks of the university. But they raise the question of presumption not on the basis of Jesus Christ, which I wish they did, but for other reasons altogether that have nothing to do with Jesus Christ. I am quite safe, therefore, in the existing, objective means of correction which I submit to and gladly welcome.

(g) Our immovable position is that Jesus Christ exists, that he has a will for everything, especially for that most important thing, the university, that the question as to his will for the university can and should be asked, that if we seek it with all our heart and mind and strength, he will, at his pleasure, reveal it to us, and that even if we do not know or find the answer, *the answer nevertheless is still there*. The lure of the existing answer is the most steadying thing. About this position there can be no possibility of presumption.

(h) Where can we be much mistaken in our judgments of the state of the mind and spirit of the university from the point of view of Jesus Christ? Are we mistaken about the materialism, naturalism, monism and self-sufficiency of the sciences? Are we mistaken about the tendency to atheism and the total absence of any reference to mystery, to something "wholly other," to something transcendent? Or are we mistaken about the dominance of subjectivism, rationalism, humanism, Freudianism, analysis, Marxism, nihilism, materialism, immanentism, monism, secularism, etc., in the humanities? Or are we raising, albeit in a preliminary fashion, false and unreal problems in this chapter? If we are not, then the will of Christ for the university is unmistakable.

(i) We know and love Jesus Christ and that is why we ask the question and seek his will for the university. Those who do not ask it either do not know him, or know him but are afraid of him, or hate him, or do not want to ask it for reasons that have nothing to do either with their own personal interests or with the substance of the question itself. But it is impossible for one who knows and loves Jesus Christ not to ask the question and seek, in fear and trembling, an answer to it.

(j) Our mistaken opinions, our misreadings of the will of Jesus Christ—our exaggerations, our extravagances, our understatements, our unguarded or careless assertions—would all be straightened out if the proposal we make in the following section should prove to be feasible and should be actually realized. We are here, in essence, only raising questions, and it is "the Institute" we are thinking of in the following section that will supply the definitive answers. The answers will correct all our errors and put to rest any possible presumption that may have afflicted us. We are persuaded that no question is more important (on this point we are on solid ground and we can never be mistaken) than the question of the state of the mind and spirit in the universities, and we are here raising the question as loudly and firmly as we can.

IV

Seventh, shall we concentrate on recapturing the great established universities for Jesus Christ, or, despairing of the task, shall we choose the line of least resistance and concentrate on establishing new Christian universities to compete with them? This is exactly the dilemma facing the Christian conscience today: to recapture or to brave out and compete.

If we concentrate on competing, two problems arise. First, the established institutions started centuries ago with as sincere an intention as ours to serve Jesus Christ; and so how do we know that we will succeed in holding out against the onslaught of secularism, rationalism, relativism, humanism, immanentism, etc., more than they did? The problem is much deeper than just to decide in good faith to go ahead and compete: the problem is the devil himself, both in the individual human heart and at large in the world.

Second, can we really compete if we start, comparatively, virtually from scratch? We cannot take too lightly the enormous headway achieved by the established institutions; we cannot overtake them, not in a hundred years; and by then, where will they be? Will we ever be able to command a library as vast and comprehensive as that of Widener, the greatest university library not only in America but in the world, which it took Harvard three centuries and a half to build up? When will we produce the authoritative treatises on history, philosophy, literature, theology, economics, government, etc., which will be adopted by the Harvards and the Stanfords and the Oxfords and the Sorbonnes and the Tübingens? When will we start competing with these schools of higher learning in the number of Nobel Prizes we will win in medicine, physics, chemistry, economics, etc.? The traditions of these universities go back for hundreds of years: Freiburg for 525 years, Harvard for 346 years. To be able really to start competing with these universities we will find ourselves obliged to use for the coming hundred years at least the very textbooks and treatises their secularist, humanist, immanentist outlook has produced. We ourselves may then gradually get secularized and humanized and immanentized.

Competing is a much more formidable task than people imagine; it may be an impossible task; it is not enough to be well-meaning and to plan to found a Christian college or university in Los Angeles or Vancouver or somewhere in Texas or Oklahoma. When, if ever, will it attain the academic stature of the existing great universities?, that is the question. Which does not mean that the hundreds of good, well-intentioned Christian colleges and universities (Protestant and Catholic) already established, or in process of being established, should be abandoned or need be discouraged. All power to them, but I do not believe they have an inkling of the character and magnitude of the challenge facing them. Or, if they do, they just shut their eyes to it.

The two horns of the dilemma, to recapture or to compete, need not be mutually exclusive. Let both carry on at the same time as best they can, but we will soon wake up to the fact that the great established universities are there and shall continue to be there; that the fledgling Christian institutions cannot compete with them nor probably attain their stature; that, impossible as the task might appear of recapturing the Harvards, the Princetons, the Yales, the Oxfords, the Sorbonnes, the Heidelbergs, for Christ, we must concentrate on this effort even more than on competing with them, especially as Christ is already at their base; and that Christ himself, the living Christ, will enable us, through lots of suffering and disappointments, provided we persevere, even if necessary for a century or more, to bring the great universities back to his embrace.

CHAPTER SEVEN

———

WHAT THEN
CAN BE DONE?

I COULD STOP RIGHT HERE. I have raised the problem in a very preliminary fashion, and that may be enough. But the question, What then can be done?, has a ringing urgency of its own. It has haunted our mind at every step in the foregoing argument.

This is a "Christian" critique of the university. We are not here to please ourselves or to serve the interests or this or that movement or ideology or culture or system of education or university; certainly we are not called upon to judge the university from the point of view of the *saecularis*. We are to seek diligently the will of Jesus Christ about the university. Jesus Christ exists and his will exists about everything. The critique focuses, then, on what Jesus Christ himself thinks of the kind of mind and spirit nurtured by the university. Jesus Christ is the principle actor and judge.

The subject is so vast and important that we could only raise the problem here. It is enough to know the university and know Jesus Christ for the problem to formulate itself at once. Merely to ask the question, What does Jesus Christ think of the university?, is to raise the problem. We elaborated some material content here and there but our treatment was altogether rough and preliminary. To get to the heart of the matter we need a deeper study and a different procedure. And the deeper study can only be accomplished through the different procedure.

From the "Christian" point of view the problem we are raising is second only to the commission laid upon the church to "earnestly contend for the faith which was once delivered unto the saints" and to evangelize the world.[1] Christ is first interested in his church, its faithfulness and its mission. But the university, as we have demonstrated, dominates the world. Can anything be more important (except Jesus Christ and his church) than the fact that our children spend between fifteen and twenty years of the most formative period of their lives either directly or indirectly under the formal influence of the university, and they and we spend the whole of our lives under its informal influence? For where in the texture of modern civilization is the university absent? The problem then, in its plenitude, is not to be raised, let alone resolved, by the writing of an essay or the delivering of a couple of lectures. What is at stake is not only the mind and spirit and character of our children, not only our own mind and spirit and character, but because of this fact, the entire fate of Western civilization and therewith the fate of the world. Nothing less than this is raised by the problem of the "Christian" critique of the university.

Let us now think of the different procedure I spoke of as a dream. But let us give the dream a name; let us call it "The Institute." I do not like the term *institute* because there are numerous and sundry institutes around, and we have in mind a task more important, more far-reaching and more historically decisive than the task of any existing institute. I can speak of a "group" or a "body" or a "circle" or a "brotherhood," but these terms are too indeterminate for the proper focusing of attention. The materially decisive character of the body which we have in mind is that it will be dedicated to monitoring the university from the standpoint of Jesus Christ. The exact name will emerge from the rough and tumble of concrete experience. The Institute, then, will itself be responsible for the elaboration in full detail of the "Christian" critique of the university. The following is a bare sketch of the outline of this dream.

The Institute in time will be governed by a fraternity of twenty-four members. Except for two or three scientists who may not be Christians, all the rest will be believing and practicing Christians, recruited, in conformity with certain criteria to be developed, from all over the Christian world. Since the only purpose of the Institute is to appraise the university from the point of view of Jesus Christ, only Christians can undertake this task, because only Christians, under the guidance of the Holy Spirit, can seek and know Christ's judgment of the university and his will for it. Neither governments nor foundations nor the secular universities could be interested in or could fulfill the purposes of the Institute: the very thought of it will embarrass them, and they will have nothing to do with it. Which does not mean that the Institute could not be associated with some university, or would refuse the help of some interested government or foundation, provided its total autonomy is preserved.

The fraternity will meet at least four times a year and preferably six. Except for their travel expenses, the members of the fraternity will receive no financial compensation from the Institute. A paid staff of thinkers, researchers and technicians will carry out the business and studies of the Institute.

I prefer the headquarters of the Institute to be Washington, but it could be also Rome or Paris.

The membership of the fraternity should include some of the most outstanding Christians of the world; in addition to their Christian faith and conduct, they should also have, or they should soon acquire, an intimate knowledge of the intellectual, moral and spiritual conditions of the university. Because of the unparalleled responsibility of the Institute, one cannot aim too high with respect to the caliber of the members. The ideal would be to include leaders and representatives from a wide range of Christian churches, as well as outstanding preachers and pastors, past or present presidents of universities or corporations, past or present heads of state, great Christian thinkers and poets, and some of the most concerned Christians.

The Institute should be independent of both church and university; but since it seeks Christ's judgment of the university, it is intimately involved in both church and university, and should therefore actively seek to develop, as much as possible, the friendliest relations with all churches and all universities; a vital desideratum that only the stature of the members who compose its fraternity can guarantee.

The mandate of the Institute is fourfold: (a) To find out, in the most authoritatively objective manner possible, the exact state of mind, morals and spirit in the universities, and to ascertain, in the most scholarly fashion possible, how it came to be what it is. (b) To let, in fear and trembling, Jesus Christ judge this existing state of mind, morals and spirit, and the way it has developed in recent centuries. (c) To consider the possibility of bringing Christ back to the university and to suggest practical ways and means to that end. (d) To consider that its mandate shall last as long as there are universities, namely, indefinitely.

No government, no foundation, no university and even no church has set up such a corporate body to concern itself exclusively and on a continuing basis with the university from this point of view. Such an institution with these purposes in mind simply does not exist and has never existed; which may mean that in the nature of the case it can never exist. And yet this is the second most important task facing mankind.

Precisely how the Institute's findings will be used, and which of these findings will be published and how they will be published, all this the fraternity of the Institute alone can decide.

The Institute should build up its endowment from Christian sources, be they churches or Christian movements or individual Christians. Its historic importance, once it is fully grasped, should be such as to call forth a broad and generous Christian response. Governments will not support it, but some foundations (for example, in the United States and Germany) may be interested. For the Institute to live up to the intellectual and spiritual expectations of the historic moment it should command a comfortable endowment. If I had three billion dollars to give away to a worthy cause, I would donate them to this project and set about seeing to it that the Institute be established. With the eminent men we have in mind composing its fraternity, if they can ever be assembled, the Institute will have the last word on every proposition made in this essay.

This is a dream, but a dream issuing from the incomparable importance of the university in the world today. The state of the mind and spirit at the university determines practically everything; hence the necessity of knowing authoritatively the exact facts of this state, and, to a Christian, what Jesus Christ thinks of these facts.

What then must be done? Nothing? Should we just rest in the dream? This is mental hedonism, as the ancient Stoics would call it. Because of the enormity of the problems (and I can think of probably double the problems that any objector can think of), shall we simply let matters drift? No thoroughgoing, grounded

Christian critique of the university? No attempt to do something about the university? But the university *is there* and Jesus Christ *is there* and the future *is there*, and both the university and the church and our children and grandchildren and the whole fate of man and civilization are crying for us to do something. No man can really comprehend what is involved here without burning to do something. The radical character of the problem and the necessity to do something impose themselves.

But no dream, no matter how compelling and well-grounded, is self-realizing. A prior feasibility study is therefore called for. The feasibility study is precisely where to begin.

This means at least four and at most six people, who have on their heart the problem of the university from the point of view of Jesus Christ, getting together and determining, from all angles and taking into account all objections and obstacles, whether the dream project of the Institute is feasible. One must move very cautiously here: it will take between three and six months to identify and assemble the members of this nucleus group, and between six months and a year afterwards for the feasibility study to be completed by them. They will be self-constituted and they will report only to themselves. They alone will decide whether their conclusions should or should not be published. If the project is not feasible, whatever the reason, if it is just fantastic, however well-meaning the dreamer or dreamers, then that is the end of the exercise. What will be gained from the exercise, however, is some deeper insight by the nucleus group into the nature and intricacies of the matter, and the knowledge that, although in the end the idea has been found wanting, it has at least been responsibly considered by this particular group. But I believe the idea is not wanting at all and if this group should fail to perceive its possibility, its reality and its necessity, another group will arise in the future who will come to the opposite conclusion.

And if the nucleus group should find that the idea is worth pursuing with a view to converting it into historical fact, then they will transform themselves from a feasibility-exploring group to the nucleus of the projected Institute itself, and will have in the meantime elaborated the character, composition, organization, purposes and functions of the Institute, and the ways of building up its endowment, in detail.

The budget of the feasibility study by the nucleus group is of the order of between a quarter of a million and half a million dollars. I think a little concentrated effort can raise this sum. No person can contribute to the feasibility study unless he already knows and loves Jesus Christ and suffers the problem of the university and the fate of Western civilization in his heart. The sources to be approached then are Christian philanthropists, wealthy churches and bulging Christian movements. I am absolutely convinced of the soundness and necessity of the idea, and if a man thinks that he is hazarding his valuable assets on a project to prove that another unproven project is or is not desirable and feasible, then let him realize that, in view of the very nature of the matter, no hazard is nobler and more rewarding than this one.

NOTES

Chapter 1: The Place & Power of the University

[1]Museums (the Metropolitan Museum of Art, the British Museum, the Hermitage, the Louvre, El Prado, etc.), public libraries (Library of Congress, New York Public Library, El Escorial, etc.) and foundations (Ford, Rockefeller, Adenauer, Volkswagen, etc.) are also great institutions, but they do not belong to the same class as the seven we listed. They are not as universal, nor, in the human interaction that transpires in them, are they as original, dynamic and determinant. Besides, the museums and libraries are government related and may be subsumed under the institution of the state, and the foundations, to the extent to which they perform educational or general national functions, fall under the university or the state.

Chapter 3: The Swerving of the Universities from their Grounding in Jesus Christ

[1]John 8:32.

Chapter 4: The Sciences

[1]John 14:6; 1:1-18; Colossians 2:9, 3; and Hebrews 1:3.
[2]Romans 1:20.
[3]Romans 1:26, 28.
[4]1 Corinthians 13:9; 3:18; and 8:1-2.
[5]Romans 10:13-15.
[6]Luke 10:22.
[7]Colossians 2:3.
[8]*Phaedo* 96A-D; 97B-99B; 100B-E. (R. Hackforth, *Plato's Phaedo* [New York: Cambridge University Press, 1972], pp. 122-34.)
[9]Job 42:5-6.

[10]Psalm 27:8-9.
[11]Acts 9:6.
[12]John 1:1, 4, 14, 17.
[13]John 11:25-26.
[14]Matthew 5:8.
[15]Acts 17:23.
[16]Ibid.
[17]Acts 17:31.
[18]Acts 17:18.
[19]*Sophist* 248E-249A. (Plato, *Sophist,* trans. Francis Macdonald Cornford [New York: The Humanities Press, 1951], p. 241.)
[20]John 14:6.
[21]Psalm 90:9-10.
[22]Psalm 90:8.
[23]Romans 5:6-8.
[24]Psalm 139:7.
[25]Job 42:5-6.

Chapter 5: The Humanities

[1]Romans 12:2.
[2]Psalm 139:7-12.
[3]The United Nations Conference on International Organization was agreed upon at Yalta on February 11, 1945, between Roosevelt, Stalin and Churchill, and was convened in San Francisco on April 25, 1945.
[4]Psalm 46:10.
[5]Exodus 3:5.
[6]See Augustine's attack on pagan demonology in his *City of God.*
[7]JP IV 4178 (X^2 A 490).
[8]Gregor Malantschuk, *The Controversial Kierkegaard,* trans. Howard V. and Edna H. Hong (Waterloo, Ontario: Wilfrid Laurier University Press, 1980), pp. 30-31.

Chapter 7: What Then Can Be Done?

[1]Jude 3.